GUIDE OF MAJORCA

131th EDITION
(23th ENGLISH EDITION)

A COLOURED MAP OF THE ISLAND

18 MAPS & PLANS

A Work declared as being in the interest of tourism
by the "Fomento del Turismo" Society for promoting
tourism in Mallorca

292 PHOTOGRAPHS IN BLACK AND WHITE
AND COLOUR BY THE AUTHOR

Editor Escalas
Santiago Rusiñol, 12 - Teléfonos 71 20 51 - 26 21 13
PALMA DE MALLORCA

Distances are given in kilometers: 1 kilometer = 0,62 miles
or 8 kilometers = 5 miles.

This GUIDE OF MAJORCA has been published in 131 editions:

ENGLISH	23	editions
FRENCH	23	»
GERMAN	19	»
SPANISH	20	»
SWEDISCH	12	»
DUTCH	15	»
ITALIAN	7	»
DANISH	9	»
FINNISH	3	»

Legal Deposit: B. 34.669-85

I.S.B.N.: 84-400-6301-6.

Editor: ESCALAS

Year 1985

Impreso por Rieusset, S. A. - Barcelona
Printed in Spain

INDEX

Prehistoric Majorca - Talaiot de *Capucorp* (*Lluchmayor*)

Prehistoric Majorca - Talaiot de *Ses Pahisses* (*Artá*).

CHAPTER I

GENERAL DESCRIPTION OF MAJORCA

PREHISTORIC MAJORCA. — The chief prehistoric period of Majorca reached its height about a thousand years before Christ; it is called by archaelogists the *Talaiot* Period from its most common and characteristic monument, the talaiot.

The talaiot is either coneshaped with a circular base, or of a foursided pyramid construction. The talaiot is a very complex structure, but these are the most common forms. They usually have one chamber, or sometimes two supported by single or double columns. The *talaiot* was, in most cases, a burial monument, as were the naveta and many of the prehistoric man-made caves which are so common on the island. As well as these two monuments, there exist also walled settlements, dolmens, fortified hills, etc., all belonging to the same period.

For their size and ease of access the following monuments are worthy of a visit: the village of *Capucorb Vell (Lluchmayor)*, the village of *Ses Pahisses (Artá)*, the village of *S'Illot (San Lorenzo)*, the burial ground of *Son Real (Ca'n Picafort)*, the talaiot of *Binifat (Sancelles)*, the caves of *Cala San Vicente (Pollensa)*, the caves of *Son Sunyer Vell (El Arenal)*, and the talaiot of *Son Danús (Santanyi)*. (J. MASCARO PASARUIS.)

Primitive Settlers. — In the transition period and approaching historical time the Majorcan Slingers became very famous for their skill. It was said, that fathers trained their sons by hanging up food in a tree and having them knock it down. This is how they had to eat. So skillful they all became that when Admiral Magón wanted to land and conquer the island he was tenaciously prevented by the Slingers in the year 205 B. C.

Roman Domination. — The island was captured first by the Phoenicians and then by the Greeks. Then in the year 123 B.C., Quinthus Cecilius Metellus, leading a powerful fleet whose ships came ready covered with hides, defeated the Majorcan Slingers, landed and put the island under Roman authority. He founded the first important cities Pollentia (now *Alcudia*), and Palmaria (now *Palma*); there is some doubt, however, whether the Roman city was situated in what today is *Puerto de Campos*, or in *Colonia de Sant Jordi*, where the sunken wrecks of Roman vessels and a large number of Roman amphora have been found in the water. The Roman theatre and the remains found in excavations in *Alcudia* are traces of this domination. At that time the population of the island numbered 30.000.

Alcudia. Roman city of *Pollentia*.

Alcudia. Roman amphitheatre.

Arab Domination. — The island was conquered by the Arabs in 902, and its reconstruction began. In 1015 it fell into the hands of Denia, recovering its independence later under the Wali of Mortadha, who turned the island into a centre for pirates who spread terror on the coasts of Cataluña, France and Italy. In 1113 an expedition to conquer the island was organized by the Catalans and the people of Pisa. This expedition, sent by Berenguer III, Count of Barcelona, consisted of 500 ships and 70.000 men. The city, *Medina Mayurca* (now *Palma*), was protected by four formidable walls, and the Arabs tenaciously resisted the attack. From the Arabs the island passed to an African "Almoravide" dynasty, who made it an independent sovereignty in 1127. After many battles, Majorca dominated North Africa, from Mogreb and Tripoli to the Sahara, for more than 50 years. The Arab domination of Majorca lasted for four centuries; its remains are the Arab Baths and the Archway of *Almudaina*, in *Palma*. Its profound effects are to be seen. too, in the way of life of the people, and in their customs and folklore.

Before the Christian conquest of the island. — The political situation between Cataluña and the Republics of Pisa and Florence was very delicate. The Catalans wanted to conquer the island and at the same time clear their coasts of pirates. The power of Arab Majorca was growing daily. Pisa, however, supported by Count Berenguer IV, was opposed to the domination of the Balearics by Génova. The Italian states, in spite of their opposed interests, established commercial links with Arab Majorca. Cataluña continued to grow in commercial and political importance, and, in spite of so many difficulties, dreamt of seizing Majorca. The rivalry between the Wali, supported by *Génova*, and *Jaime I*, the count-king of Cataluña grew stronger every day, reaching its peak in 1227.

The Feast of Tarragona. — Where the seed of the conquest was sown. The great seafarer Pere Martell, on the 16th of November 1228, invited the King and the great nobles to a magnificent feast. After serving them with rich delicacies, the host gave a superb description of Majorca, which he knew from his frequent visits, and to interest them in its products, he gave them Majorcan olives with the dessert. In this manner he enraptured and inflamed all those who were present.

Consequences of the Feast. — A short time after, the King who was only twenty years old, summoned a gathering in *Barcelona* of all his noblemen-at-arms, and to give it a democratic character, he invited the commoners of *Cataluña*. The gathering was held in the Sala del Tinell in the old royal palace. Gathering afterwards in the *Cortes*, the young King had overcome the arguments of the Aragonese that they should first march against

Murcia. They all volunteered their share in the venture, each suplying both military necessities (men, arms and horses), and money. The Cortes disbanded on Christmas Eve 1228, taking the oath with cries of "To Majorca! To Majorca!" The volunteers enlisted and all *Cataluña* burned with enthusiasm.

The Military Expedition. — On the 5th of September 1229, all difficulties solved, the expedition was put to sea. The landing-force consisted of four corps, 16.000 men, and 1.500 horses, carried in 150 large ships and other smaller ones. The Wali of Majorca, forewarned of the attack, had ready an army of 18.000 men and 1.000 horses. The King Jaime I was in the first ship, commanding the formidable fleet. On the following day they came in sight of the island. On the 7th the first soldiers landed on the islet of Pantalaleu, near *La Dragonera,* and established a bridgehead. The main body of the army landed in *Santa Ponsa* on the 10th. Faced with such a dangerous situation the Wali came to meet them with 5.000 men, but another contingent had landed at *La Porrassa* in order to surround them.

Fall of the City. — The first encounters favoured the Catalans, due to numerous defections among the Arabs. Continuing the struggle, the royal army achieve the position, 5 kms. to the North of the city, which has since been called *El Secar de La Real.* It was here where the assault on the city was planned, culminating with the breaking of the wall and the victorious entry of King Jaime I at the head of his army, on the 31st of December 1229.

Foundation of the Kingdom of Majorca. — Immediately after the Conquest (in March 1230), Jaime I founded the new State of Majorca, publishing the Carta de Població which laid down the democratic base of equality, liberty and autonomy. In its 37 chapters it gives details of Justice with independent tribunals, political-administrative standards, both civil and criminal, and for new settlers, free property, commercial expansion inviolability of homes, ovens, mills and ships. It laid down the Powers of the Government, and the foundation, by a system of representation, of the Gran i General Consell. The "Baile" was responsible for order and for the fulfilment of Royal commands, and the "Verguer" for everything connected with civil and criminal justice. Together they provided the most advanced constitution of those times.

The Kingdom of Majorca. Reign of Jaime II. — In 1276 Jaime I died, leaving to his son Jaime II the kingdoms of Majorca, Rosellón and Montpeller. The King concentrated most of his energies on the island, and he achieved a great deal. Although it is widely believed that it was the Conqueror who promised to build the cathedral, it was in fact Jaime II who put into effect

the construction of this magnificent monument, and began the building. He built the Royal Palace of *Almudaina* on the site of the Wali's palace, and at the same time the palace of *Perpinya*, in a similar style. The castle of *Bellver* is one of his works, a building both military and palacial, as well as the royal palaces of *Valldemosa* (on the site now occupied by the Cartusian Monastery), and those at *Sineu* and *Manacor*. He built the walls at *Alcudia* and founded many settlements (*Lluchmayor, Manacor, Petra, Felanitx*, etc.).

With regard to culture, Jaime II was the great patron of Ramón Llull, the greatest figure of the times. The shape of the city changed enormously with the opening of new roads within it. The huge churches which are now the parish churches of *San Miguel, Santa Eulalia, San Jaime, San Nicolás* and *Santa Cruz* were begun. Among the monasteries and convents to be founded were *Santa Margarita* and *San Francisco*, which are today national monuments. He was unable to achieve the diversion of the river "La Riera", which caused so many floods, outside the city. In the field of trade, he improved the navy and established the currency of his kingdom. Socially he established minimum wages for agricultural workers.

The Reign of Sancho. — He inherited the throne in 1311 on the death of his father Jaime II. He developed even further everything achieved by his predecessor in trade and in civil law, confirming the liberties and privileges granded by Jaime II.

He admitted high military expenditure in the face of the threat of aggression by neighbouring states, until the signing of the peace treaty with the king of Bujía in 1312. He died in 1324, and with his death began he decline in splendour of the Majorcan monarchy.

End of the Monarchy in Majorca. — King Sancho died childless, leaving the throne to his nine year old nephew, who was Jaime III. The kingdom placed itself under the protection of a Regency Council who loyal to their king, tried to maintain its integrity and the progress already made. Among other things it founded in 1325 the *Consulado de Mar*. Then began the struggle between Majorca and the King of Aragon, Pedro III, brother-in-law to Jaime III, who wished to take possession of Majorca, and in fact succeeded. Jaime III tried to regain it, and organized an invasion force, but he was defeated and killed in the battle of *Lluchmayor* on the 25th of October 1349. With his death, Majorca was firmly annexed to the kingdom of Aragon. Aragon and Castilla united and conquered Granada in 1492, thus founding the national and political unit of Spain, of which Majorca has since been a part. Today, together with the other islands of Menorca and Ibiza, it forms the Spanish province of Baleares. (From "The History of Majorca". *Mo. Antoni Pons.* 1963.)

← *Palma.* Arab baths.

Palma. Arab Arch of *S'Hort del Rei.*

GEOGRAPHICAL DESCRIPTION. — Majorca is 3.640 km.² in extent. Its coast line extends about 300 km. The whole population of the island is 534.000, that is to say 147 to a km² The island has the form of a rhomboid with three large bays: *Palma, Alcudia* and *Pollensa.* The three are full of beauty. Majorca offers two zones: the plain *(Es Pla)* and the mountains *(Sa Muntanya).* The mountains occupy the northern part from NE. to SW. running parallel to the coast. The chain is about 100 kms. long with 6 to 12 kms. broad on the average. The chain extends from *La Dragonera* (separated by the *Freu*), extreme west point of the island, to *Formentor Cape,* which is the extreme northern point. The highest peak is *Puig Mayor* attaining 1.500 metres. The northern ridge is called *La Serra* and it occupies the fifth of the total extent of the island.

The plain *(Es Pla)* covers the southern part of the island; it is devoted to agriculture. Its great fertility is owed to its situation, because the northern mountains give great protection from the violent gales. The surface is level and low and makes possible the subterranean water supply. Around *Palma* at *Sant Jordi* as well as *La Puebla* one can see mills with motors

Palma. Cathedral. Presbitery.

by hundreds. On this part of the island mountains are scarce and low. There are *Randa* at *Lluchmayor; Bonany* at *Petra; San Salvador* at *Felanitx* and *Ca'n Ferrutx* at *Artá;* they scarcely attain 500 metres.

The capital of the island is *Palma* (290.00). It is the centre of the ways of communication and of activities. The principal towns include *Manacor* (24.000), *Inca* (18.000). Both are capitals of districs. *Felanitx* (13.000), *Sóller* (10.000), *Lluchmayor* (13.000), *Pollensa* (10.500) and *La Puebla* (10.000). Some others less important not attaining 10.000 are. *Artá, Andraitx, Sineu, Petra, Campos,* etc. All these smaller towns are agricultural centres. A net of roads and railroads connect *Palma* and nearly all towns to each other.

GEOLOGY. — The Balearic Islands form the only group situated in West Mediterranean. They are not at all of volcanic origin as commonly stated. They are formed in great part of calcareous and sandy rocks, clay and marl. It is obvious that these materials were formed in the bottom of disappeared sea or in continental lagoons, as in the case of Majorcan lignites.

All that means a long geologic history starting in the island of Menorca, where evidence of primery of Paleozoic terrains are present. It continues in the other islands where we can see testimonies of the second and terciary epochs.

Nevertheless both groups have a different origin. In the Balearic islands we can discriminate an old group with *Menorca* and a more recent one: *Ibiza-Mallorca*. That occurs because its evolution was different.

Ibiza-Mallorca were born by orogenic forces which raised the huge mountains of Penibética chain from Cádiz to *La Nao* Cape in *Alicante*. They are the extreme west point. Their rocky materials rose from an immense grave which ran in the same direction as the mountain of today. It was a pressing force on the sediments, performed by the northern part of Africa. It compressed the old sea muds against the stiff and ancient mass of the Iberian Plateau, like the bellows of an accordion.

In this way *Ibiza* and Majorca saw the sunshine, at the same epoch when the Alps and other mountains of Europe were born.

This is the reason that all their eminencies are young and whimsical, in form of long parallel and broken chains like the waves of sea breaking against the beach.

In the first time the mountains of Majorca and *Ibiza* were bound with the zone Alicante my means of a large stratum of sediments (Middle Miocene).

In the course of time, gradually through the forces both of sea and vertical movements, began the progress of separation from the mainland to end in the actual situation. (Extract from "Biogeografía de las Baleares", G. Colom, 1957.)

MAJORCAN LITERATURE. — Although the official language of Spain is Castellan which is known and correctly spoken by 95 % of Majorca people the Majorcan language based on the Catalan is the native tongue of the island. This language is derived from the Latin and was introduced by the Catalan people who established themselves in Majorca after its conquest by King James I in 1229, taking the place of the arab tongue which was spoken by the inhabitants under the Moslem rule.

The Catalan tongue was still going through a period of formation when the greatest Majorcan that have known the centuries, Ramón Llull (1231-1315), brought it to its fullness. After being a steward for the King of Majorca Jaime II, he became an apostle of the Christian faith in the year 1262. His Christian impulse was to spread christianity all over the world. He wrote

Cathedral. Main Door, *La Almoina*.

more than 250 books, most of them in Catalan. He was a mystic phylosopher, poet and novelist. Among his most important works in Catalan are: *Llibre de la contemplació, Blanquerna, Félix de les merevelles* and *Arbre de la Ciencia*. Here is a quotation from Menéndez Pelayo that says: "The first philosophy ever heard was in Catalan, from the mouth of Ramón Llull".

In the XIV, XV, XVI, centuries made his appearance, the notable Fra Anselm Turmeda (1355-1423) Franciscan who became a Mahomedan, and author of *Profecies, Disputació d'un ase* and *Cobles de la divisió del regne de Mallorque*. Other poets are Guillem de Torrella and Jaume d'Olesa. The most notable was Francesc d'Olesa who died in 1550, author of *La nova art de trobar* and *Obra del menyspreu del món*. In the XVI century the Majorcan literature like the Catalan went through a period of desintegration by the intensification of the Castellan influence, being the reason for the works of no reknown written in Majorca. In 1715 the Majorcan tongue lost its official character, staying pure since then, in common with its people and literature.

Shortly after the initial Catalan Renaissance in 1833, the Majorcan literature was reborn. Tomás Aguiló, Montis and Quadrado colaborated for the weekly edition *La Palma* (1840) still

16

Palma. Fisherman's wharf. →

Palma. Gardens of *S'Hort del Rei*. →

Cathedral. Museum.

written in Castellan. Of these only Tomás Aguiló (1812-1883), cultivated with success the revived poetry which, little by little was incorporated with the Catalan under the aspect of litera- ture. The Majorcan poet, folklorist and philologist Mariano Aguiló was principally responsible for the restoration of the language, he published the *Romance feudal* and the first cla- sical *Diccionari Catalá*. It was notable, the poetical contributions of Josep Lluís Pons i Gallarza (1823-1894), Jeroni Rosselló (1827-1909), Guillem Forteza (1838-1898), Tomás Forteza (1838- 1898) who besides the cultivation of poetry published the first Scientific *Gramática Catalana* and Ramón Pico Campanar (1843- 1906) author of notable romances of knighthood. Pere d'Alcán- tara Penya (1823-1906) and Bartomeu Ferrá (1843-1924) were popular play writers of the customs and habits of the time. Gabriel Maura brother of the politician Antonio Maura was a remarkable prosaist, his work *Aigoforts* describes with in- tense colour the life of Majorca, in the second half of the XIX century.

The majorcan poetry arrived at its fullness with the con- tribution of the topmost authors: Mossèn Miguel Costa i Llobe- ra (1854-1922) and Joan Alcover (1854-1926). The former, with a deep clasical culture not only did he produce poems of great value but he gave new forms to the Catalan language. Joan Al- cover, besides being an important author and poet, published

Cathedral. Details of the *Mirador* Doorway.

his *Elegies*, worthy to figure in the universal anthology. To these two poets followed Miguel dels Sants Oliver (1864-1920) who besides being a poet was a great publisher and historian; María Antonia Salvá (1870-1958) who enriched the literature by her personal notes of great humanist and prose writer; Miguel Ferrá (1855-1947) with his fine aristocratic style, purified and raised Majorcan poetry. Among other poets, must be mentioned; Mateu Obrador (1853-1909); Josep María Tous Maroto (1870-1949); Gabriel Alomar (1873-1941); Joan Ramis d'Aireflor (1882-1956) and Bartomeu Forteza (1894-1957). As a prose writer, Mossèn Antoni M.ª Alcover (1862-1932) who collected the *Rondalles Mallorquines* (folktales) and initiated the great work, the *Diccionari Català-Valencià-Balear* which was completed in 1962. And the prose writer Mossèn Salvador Galmes, eminent follower of Ramón Llull (1878-1951).

Besides the mentioned writers, a great number of reknown, literary men in the fields of poetry, novels and the Majorcan theatre cultivate the verse in its most divers tendencies and forms. The first innovator of poetry was Bartomeu Rosselló Porcel (1913-1937). (MIGUEL FORTEZA).

Cathedral. Sepulchre of Bishop Galiana.

Doorway to old choir.

THE MAJORCA SAILING TRADE. — In the history of Majorca the sailing trade plays an important part. We shall make an extract of the findings of Sr. LLABRES BERNAL. In the XII century soon after the conquest of Mallorca and at the beginning of the Christian Era, the island, the commercial marine developed in the way of its commerce. The initial port of *Palma* was *Porto Pi* with defended entrances by two towers connected by chains. One of these towers "Pelaires" (XV century) is actually preserved intact, today dominating the entrance to the jetty for liners. The navigation acquired such importance that it became necessary to build a new port starting from the actual *Lonja*.

At the end of the XV century began the decline of the shipping commerce and consequently that of the marine, partly due to the adverse circumstances suffered by the island and the wars of the time; this decline occured at the same time as the opening of the new routes after the discovery of America. The 300 boats that formed the marine at the time was reduced gradually in the course of the XV century.

← Cathedral. Interior.

Sepulchre of Bishop Torrella.   Capitulary hall.

The rebirth of the merchant navy in the XVIII century was building up until it reached its peak in the XIX century. The navigation and specially the trade of olive oil, fabrics and other products of the island influenced the other side of the Atlantic, Antille, and the Caribe with prosperity, prefering the port of Havana. In the other direction towards Philipines by the Cape of Good Hope. The journeys lasted months some times more than a year, carried out by boats which tonnage varied between 100 and 200 tons.

During this period the island was frequenty assaulted by the Barbary pirates who did some sacking and kidnapping and then demanded high ransoms. These disasters went on affecting the trade until one day, in the middle of the XVIII century, a skipper named Antonio Barceló, *Es Capità Antoni*, decided to stop it. With an armed squadrom of "Jabeques" (typical boats of special latin sail of great speed), he was able to carry out his mission, cleaning with success the Mediterranean of sea pirates. He was well praised for his courage and was condecorated Lieutenant of the Royal Marine. The security of shipping was absolute after 1830 with the conquest of Argelia by France.

← Cathedral. Pulpit.

Santa Eulalia   *San Nicolás.*

During the XIX century we enjoyed a great splendor in spite of the competition that began to be made by the steam sailing boats, in 1833 the first regular line between Palma and Barcelona was established, it did not last too long and at the end of 1837 began the service the "Mallorquín" paddle steamer, the first of this kind to be registered in Palma. In face of this competition the sailing ships increased by number and tonnage. In the middle of the century its number reached 140 nearly all built in Majorca in local shipyards under the plans and direction of the experts of the place with craftsmanship. The ship owners, as well as the crew who maintained the trade and communications of Spain and Majorca by all the seas and continents was over.

At the end of the XIX century the last of the Spanish colonies was lost and because of the progress of the steamships the definite decline of the sailing ships began, and now definitely could not recover. Still, during the first European War (1914-1918) because of how valuable the ships became during war time some ships were built in Mallorca but their destiny was to be very different from those which preceeded them. The glorious historical mission which united for so many centuries the flags of Spain and Majorca by all the seas and continents was over.

Church of *Santa Margarita*.

MAJORCAN ARCHITECTURE. — It is very difficult to achieve a synthesis of this architecture, whose artistic significance has had moments of real importance in the history of art, spreading beyond the limits of the island in the XIV and XV centuries. A complete study must be divided under at least four headings: religious, military, civil and domestic.

Religious Architecture. — This reaches its peak in the centuries of Gothic art, as the Romanesque was already declining by the time of the Christian conquest of Jaime I (1229); and within these centuries, to the years of the independent monarchy of Majorca. Famous examples of the Majorcan Gothic architecture are the Cathedral, *Santa Eulalia* and *San Francisco*, all three products of the great cultural and economic progress of the independent monarchy of Majorca. In the Baroque period, especially in the XVIII century, Majorcan art reaches a new splendour in a few isolated churches —the best of these being *San Antonio de Viana*, in *Palma*— and in the many altarplaces which enrich the churches.

Military Architecture also dates from the time of the Majorcan Kings. Its most interesting monuments are the castle of *Bellver* and the palace of *Almudaina* (closely connected with the Royal Palace at *Perpiñán*), the walls of *Alcudia*, now being restored, and the fortified castles, of which the most important is *Santueri (Felanitx)*.

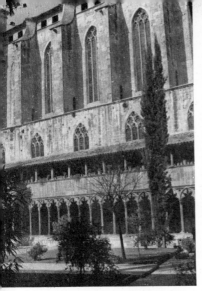

San Francisco. Lateral façade

Presbitery.

Civil Architecture has one fundamental example to the history of Gothic art: the *Lonja* in *Palma*, an expression of maritime power in the city, the exchange and commercial centre between Italy and the Atlantic ports. Its creator, Guillermo Sagrera, is the centre of a school of architecture, who working in Rosellón, Naples and in Sicily, determines the only moment in the history of art in which Spain influences Italy and not the reverse.

The Domestic Architecture of Majorca has two aspects, both equally interesting, noble architecture and popular architecture. The first is best expressed in the large palaces of the nobility, to be found in the city, built between the XIV and XVIII centuries, in styles ranging from gothic to late baroque, and also the country estates, built in the Italian style, and without equal in the Península. The gardens are very beautiful and there survives in them, by some phenomenon, the moorish-oriental spirit. The popular architecture of Majorca is clearly influenced by the Greek, the Roman and the Italian. It is functional, aesthetically suitable to the landscape, and it has a harmony with nature, contrasting with the architecture of Menorca and Ibiza, which has a strong eastern flavour (due in part to their covered terraces and whitewashed walls). The Majorcan type often has a covered central patio with curved tiles and rubble-work walls of natural stone. (ANTONIO J. ALOMAR, Architect.)

La Almoina house.

Roses house window. *San Jaime* street.

COMMUNICATIONS. — The island has plenty of communications with the world, both by air and sea. It has magnificent ports (air and sea ports) with modern buildings.

There are regular and daily services of steamers with Barcelona (except on Sundays). And a three times a week service with Alicante and twice a week with Valencia. There are liners to Marseille and Algiers as well as to Italian ports, North of Europe, North America.

We have air lines with daily services to Barcelona, Madrid, Valencia, Marseille, Algiers, Paris, Geneve, Bruselles, Amsterdam, London-intensified during Summer.

The communications between the islands are served by steamers twice a week Palma - Ibiza, weekly Palma - Mahón, Palma - Ciudadela. There is an air service Palma - Mahón.

This net of communications makes it possible for the visitors to have a choice of combinations to come to our island.

Façade of the Episcopal Palace.

AGRICULTURE. — The main fountain of wealth of Majorca is agriculture. Land property is very much divided. There are no more huge estates in the island and most of the labores till their own soil. Brunnes has said: "Majorcans are hard workers above all". A Frenchman, who lived in Majorca for many years would say: "Here children work like women; women work like men, and men work like Titans".

Farming is intense. There are so many trees in this island that Queen Alexandra of England once said: "One can walk here from tree to tree across the whole island." The most important produce is almonds. An average almond harvest reaches 7.000.000 kgs. Main agricultural products are carots, figs, dried apricots, potatoes, vegetables, pigs, rabbits and fowls. Wines of *Binisalem* and *Felanitx* have got a good renown. Excellent oil is produced in *Sóller* and *Buñola*. Almonds, dried apricots and figs are largely exported. In May the first potatoes of *La Puebla* are exported directly to England.

Staircase of *Casa Oleo* (*La Almudaina* street).

FAMOUS VISITORS. *Writers.* — The literature produced by famous writers about the island is both extensive and varied. We refer to those who have explored it and have left us their impressions in books. In the XIX century we have Grasset de St. Sauver, who in 1801 published "Journeys in the Balearic Isles". George Sand, accompanied by Chopin, visited in 1833, publishing the following year her famous book "Un Hiver à Majorque", a book which although it reflects in one part bitterness, it also gives a superb description of the island landscape. In 1840, J. B. Laurens published "Souvenir d'un Voyage d'Art à l'Île de Majorque", a painter's description with many of the author's original drawings. Juan Cortada, after exploring the whole island, by way of the mountain roads, gives a complete picture of the island in his diary "Journey on the Island of Majorca in the summer of 1845". Ramón Medel, in 1849, published his "Traveller's Manual of Palma, Majorca"; this was perhaps the first guide-book we had in Majorca, with a full description of the city, its monuments and its fortifications. His impressions of the city of those times, of which he describes the atmosphere, are quite exciting. In 1867 Pagenstecher published "The Island of Majorca. Description of a Journey". He describes it as he discovers it. He landed at *Alcudia* and thanks to a cart that he met he was able to move to *Palma*, where he arrived and spent the night. He had trouble finding somewhere

La Lonja. Exterior & Interior.

to sleep. He went right round the island on horseback and describes it, sometimes as a traveller sometimes as a naturalist.

At the end of the XIX century (1893) Gaston Vuillier published a magnificent work, carefully edited by Hachette, "Les Iles Baléares". He describes it, with remarkable improvement in communications, in a transition period, now using stage-coaches, carriages, and the "modern" railway; he praises the lodging of the *Miramar (Ca Madó Pilla)* and the facilities of the Archduke. And to complete the XIX century we must make a special mention of H. R. H. Ludwig Salvador, Archduke of Austria. He was really enchanted with Majorca, and this enchatment made him publish and edit himself, at the end of the XIX century leaving a veritable library of magnificently presented editions. He left not one corner unvisited nor one detail unstudied. Such costly editions with magnificent illustrations, he later presented to the libraries of Europe. In this century, into a historical work, such has been the transformation of the island, that today, not even Rusiñol would recognize it.' Unamuno, Salaverría, Sanchis Sivera, Azorín, Rubén Darío, all published magnificent articles, after collected in books. These are the footsteps, the unforgetable memories of their passing through the island.

32

Palma. Cathedral. →
Palma. *La Lonja.* →
The cathedral. →

In 1912 Jules Leclercq published "Voyage à l'Île Majorque", and Marie de Behen, her "Diary" of her journey, which is pleasant and original both in its text and in the author's original photographs. In 1925 Mrs. Chamberlain published her "Guide to Majorca", which helped to make the island popular in Great Britain. In 1928 Mr. Byne published a great volume with many engravings, drawings and plans, "Majorcan houses and gardens", in which he studies with all the skill of a great architect the Majorcan manor house, both in the city and the country. 1932 is notable for the book "Majorque" by Francis de Miomandre, and "Baleares, Iles heureuses" by Fayol. This gives a marvellous description of all the stored up art of the city and the islands; and the choice of illustrations are of equal stature.

Such a profusion of books and works, of which we have quoted only a few of the most important, shows the importance which the island has always had. All fullfil a historical mission: to make Majorca known, a mission for which Majorca could never repay them in a manner which is worthy of them.

Artists. — For a long time Majorca has been the Mecca of artists. They are attracted by the variety of colours and light. They have helped to make her wellknown, but she too has helped them to fame, supplying an unique landscape, varied as it is from high mountain, plains, creeks and pines, fantastic vegetation of olive trees, almonds in bloom, typical scenes, etc. They can be found in all the galleries of Europe. Among the great men who came to paint Majorca we name Mir, Santiago Rusiñol, Anglada Camarasa, Bernaregi, Citadini, etc., and many others whose stays in the island were shorter.

← Cathedral. Presbitery.

← Cathedral. Silver candelabra.

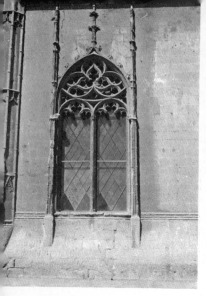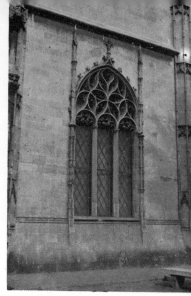

La Lonja - windows.

INDUSTRY. — There are no large industrial centres in the island, but the manufacture of shoes has some importance *(Palma, Lluchmayor, Inca, Binisalem, Lloseta)*. We find textile industry *(Palma* and *Sóller)*; artificial pearls' *(Manacor* and *Felanitx)*; sausages *(Felanitx, Manacor, Sóller)*; chemical fertilizers *(Palma)*. The industry of embroideries has a large development as well as furniture manufacture.

FOLK-LORE. — The typical Majorcan costume has quite disappeared. At the beginning of this century it was still worn in the villages. Majorcan folk-lore had been renewed with to-day's tourism. Now our folk-lore has a new life in professional groups in public performances. These groups have great international success. Some are quite remarkable like those of *Valldemosa, Sóller, Petra* and *Selva.*

GASTRONOMY. — Majorcan cooking has its own qualities and personality. For example we may point out *escaldums*, a special dish of turkey and poultry. *Caldera*, particular dish of fish. There are excellent sausages, like *sobrassada*. Among the Majorcan pastry we have the delicious *panades, coquerrois, doblegats, robiols, cuartos, coxins* and the *ensaimada* of worldwide renown.

Window of the convent of the church *La Concepción* (XV century). →

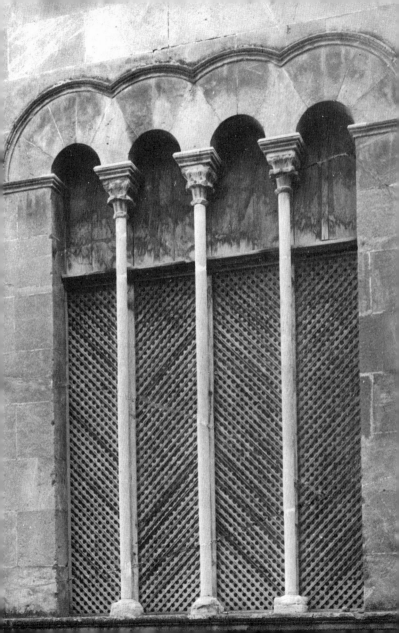

View of *La Almudaina* palace.

CLIMATE AND HEALTH. — Majorca would have never become a so important tourist resort without having a climate so excellent as it has. Ours is a true Mediterranean climate. E. Martionne describes it as "temperated climates without cold season, and with great luminosity". The eminent French geographer J. Brunnes, who visited our island said, it is all the Mediterranean world that dared her clean sky and roughness of her mountains with Central, West and North Europe. There are not few resemblances between the climate and the forms of vegetation, animal and human life in this Mediterranean land. Vital energy is here intense. Here one can find all forms of vegetation shrubs and other greens as well as plants which endure summer drought.

Without great changes the average temperature is 25° cent. in Summer and 10° in Winter. The average temperature in the year is 17'7°. Relative dampness is 68'8 % corresponding to a reasonable dry climate.

Prevailing winds are from S. that is to say: temperate winds. The long chain of mountains shelters the island against the cold winds from the north.

Rainfall is uncommon in Spring and Summer. Maximum occurs in November and December. The average about 477 mm. yearly. The extent of the coast with the sea winds soften the temperature during the night: the daily change is not over 8° cent.

Cloudless sunny days are more than 170 in number during a year. The diaphaneity of air and the sunshine give all sorts of colours and shades to our landscapes.

It is seldom foggy (4 to 5 days in the year). Days with rainfall are also few (75 in the year). It is very frequent to see in these days the sun shining after the rain.

The different elevation above the sea level causes little local variations, which afford climatic changes. There are points like *Valldemosa* or *Lluch* situated 400 metres above the sea level. These variations can be very useful for climate treatment.

The excellent climatic conditions are very propitious for healthiness. There are no indiguenuous or endemic diseases. Mortality was 11'21 per 1.000 in 1953, in short: a perfect health.

HOTELS.—Majorca counts today with all kinds of lodgings, from the economic pension to the most luxurious hotels on the beaches, around the town, amids the woods. Visitors can make their choice according to their preferences. With more than 180.000 beds, tourists are sure to find good lodging even in summer, the highest tourist season.

AIR AND SEA TRAFFIC. — The island posseses the large port of *Palma* of modern construction, and from the touristic point of view one of the most important of the Mediterranean. At its docks, with the maritime station tie up the largest transatlantic liners. It receives courtesy visits from foreign fleets (English, French, Italien, U.S.A., Dutch, Portuguese, etc.). A visit to the port of Palma is included in all the Mediterranean cruises. Besides, it is linked by regular service with the most important European ports, also with Africa and America. With all these services more than 150 ships of large tonnage bring in over 100.000 passengers to *Palma*.

Less important ports are those of *Andraitx, Sóller, Pollensa, Cala Ratjada, Porto Cristo* and *Porto Colom*. Outstanding in importance is the port of *Alcudia*, nearby is the central electric plant, which serves most of the island. This port facilitates anchorage to the larger ships.

The international airport of *Son Sanjuan* at 9 kms. from *Palma* with runaways of 4 kms. maintains regular services with direct flights to all important aerodromes of Europe and North Africa.

During the year 1981 the volume of sea traffic was as follows:
Incoming ships 3.661 with a total of 14.264.515 tons and 395.977
    passengers.
Outgoing ships 3.659 with a total of 14.185.970 tons and 355.977
    passengers.
This means a total volume of 7.320 ships, 28.371.954 tons and
    751.746 passengers.
249 cruisers pulled up at *Pelaires* docks.
The international airport of *Son Sanjuan* registered the following
    traffic in 1980.
36.641 aircraft inbound with 3.631.957 passengers.
36.677 aircraft outbound with a total of 3.670.822 passengers.
Total volume of air traffic during 1980 was 73.318 planes and
    7.302.779 passengers.

In both the port and airport of Palma there was a grand total during 1980 of 8.428.692 passengers.

Doorway & interior of the Diocesan Museum.

TOURISM. — Majorca is now a touristic resort well known in the world. Our island is visited by people of all nations. Some of them come here to tour the island, others prefer to spend part of their life; but all tourists enjoy the beauty of the landscapes of our island. They seek characteristic strokes or the charm of our town. *Palma* keeps monumental features but at the same time it is modern and can offer perfect comfort and tourist organization. Those who visit our island talk about our island, and every day, articles about Majorca are published in journals all over the world. The most famous painters in the world come here to perpetuate on their canvas the wonder of the Majorcan sun and colours.

Over three million foreign visitors come here every year. The number of travellers who arrive in Majorca on the ships entering the port of *Palma* is over 300.000.

CHAPTER II

PALMA AND ITS ENVIRONS

I.—HISTORY OF THE CITY

The first news we have relating to the foundation of the city goes back to the time of the conquest of the island by the Romans. These founded the colonies of *Palmaria* and *Pollentia* (to-day *Palma* and *Alcudia*, respectively). Vandals and Goths destroyed these towns and it is not until the Saracens conquered the island in the eighth century that the true history of the city begins, it being named *Medina Mayurca* and situated in the same place as now.

It was the Arab capital for four centuries. In the twelfth century it had four concentric, walled precincts, with their towers and moats. The arch of *La Almudaina*, all that remains of the fortifications, was one of the gates of the citadel. The palace-castle of *La Almudaina* was the residence of the Wali.

The conquest of the city by the Christian Catalonians changed its life and constitution, the Arab style being replaced by the Gothic. King James I, the Conqueror, endowed it with a constitution of its own, creating the *Great* and *General Council* for its government and care of economic questions, an institution which lasted until the War of Succession, during which it was abolished when the house of Bourbon began to reign in 1714. For its administration he created the jury, composed of six individuals chosen by drawing lots as representatives of the different estates of social classes. The king exercised legislative and judicial power, delegating its attributions to the governors, to the bailiff general of the city and to those of the towns. In 1325 the Sea Consulate, *Consulado de Mar* a tribunal with jurisdiction over maritime affairs, was created.

Church of *Santa Catalina de Sena*　　　　　　　Church of *Montesión*.

During the 15th. century the city suffered many calamities. The stream called *La Riera* crossed the city and divided it geographically into two parts, the upper of *La Almudaina* of Levant and the lower, the *Villa* or Occident. The old bed of the stream (or torrent), which later constituted a serious danger for the city's inhabitants, is what to-day has become a spacious avenue, a kilometre and a half long, which runs from the Instituto along the boulevards called *La Rambla* and *El Borne*, to end at the boulevard named *Paseo de Sagrera*, where the stream (the "torrente") had its outlet. It was King James II of Majorca who in 1303, gave the first order for the stream's course to be changed, a task which was not realised until 1623, in which year it was diverted to the moat of the city wall, along which it passes since then. Among the numerous catastrophes occasioned by the overflowings of its banks which occurred in October of 1403 deserves special mention. This demolished the lower part of the city, causing more than 5.000 victims.

In 1451 occurred the famous struggle between aliens and citizens. The city was besieged by the rebels. There were lootings everywhere, destructions and crimes, until an armed force arrived from Naples and re-established normality, executing the

Entrance to *La Portella*   *Montenegro* street.

principal instigators. During this same century the rivalries
existent between the families of the Majorcan aristocracy were
intense and gave rise to continuous struggles and challenges,
sometimes for the most trivial reasons. One of the most serious
took place in the church of San Francisco on the 2nd. of November of the year 1490 between the rival houses *Armadans*
and *Espanyols*, who without respect for the sacred building nor
for the religious act which was being celebrated there, passed
from insults to a bloody battle involving more than 300 persons,
with dead and wounded on both sides, it being necessary to ex-
hibit the figure of Christ crucified to appease the fury of the
fighters and put an end to the terrible battle. At the end of
this century the *Estudio General* was founded, a study centre
that has played such a decisive part in the cultural development
of the city.

When the island came to form part of the Kingdom of Aragon, Palma continued to be the capital, being the seat of the
political and military authority of the island, with governors
dependent directly of the King and preserving its constitution
and autonomy with the *Great and General Council*, the jurors
of the city and the syndics. The palace-castle *La Almudaina*
became the residence of the Viceroy, representative of the central power.

← Street and convent of *La Concepción*.

View of *La Portella* city district.

Palace *Marqués de Casa La Torre.*

In the 16th century, when the unity of Spain was already a reality, the *Germania* movement spread throughout the island. The city lived days of terror and barbarism, the Germanised elements occupying the University (now the Town Hall). The arrival of the royal troops, however soon liquidated the revolt and the main leaders, headed by Francisco and Juanot Colom, were executed.

It was during the XVI and XVII centuries that the nobility of Majorca was formed with the families coming from the country who made their residence in *Palma*. The town has the same appearance as in the previous centuries, narrow streets, doorways with pointed arches, double arched windows *(finestres coronelles)* with gargoyles, that later on were covered with sloping roofs with long eaves; a lot of them can still be seen now-a-days. The Lonja, was already operating; it is an illustration of the commercial wealth of that period. The town as a whole looked like one of the Middle Ages.

During the 17th century the city suffered many calamities. A great drought gave rise to famine and in 1652 an outbreak of plague caused great devastation. By order of King Philip IV work on the city walls was begun, the costs falling on the University and the Royal Patrimony. The work was carried out under great economic difficulties and suffered many interruptions.

Consulado de Mar.

During the 18th century there was a profound political transformation due to the consequences of the so-called war of succession between the houses of Austria and of Bourbon. Until then the city had preserved its privileges, liberties and exemption from taxes. Now Palma declared itself partisan of the Austrias. After the taking of Barcelona on the 11th September, 1714, the troops of Philip V occupied the island and besieged the city, which surrendered. The new king abolished all the autonomy it had enjoyed for centuries, suppressing the *Great and General Council*, the jurors and all else that had its beginnings in the concessions made by James I on the basis of the conquest. He (Philip V) created the Municipality of Palma, constituted by councillors with restricted powers, who could not use the toga and whose appointment, instead of being by lot, among the different social scales, was made by the king.

During the 19th century the city suffered the same political ups and downs as were produced on the mainland. At the beginning of the century the Tribunal of the Inquisition was definitely abolished. In 1837 the convent and church of Santo Domingo, magnificent Gothic monuments, were demolished. The

Palma. Flower market in *La Rambla* (Vía Roma).

Palma. Promenade of General Franco (once Borne).

Door of the old city wall   Chapel of Consulado.

city suffered three epidemics, that of yellow fever in 1821, that of the cholera in 1865 and once again that of yellow fever in 1870. At the beginning of the century the city walls were finished, but, in 1873, the part of the mole situated in what is now the *Paseo de Sagrera* was already falling down.

In this same 19th century were begun the internal reforms which were to have so much repercussion on those realised later. With *La Riera* deviated, a large square was left free, in which were held the great festivals, tournaments, military parades and so on and through which circulated the great horse-drawn carriages of the epoch. By initiative of the Captain General the Municipality built the boulevard *El Borne*, placing stone benches along it as well as trees and potted plants and at its end the four figures *Ses Lleones*. In 1833 the fountain *Las Tortugas* was installed. This still exists, although modified, and gave rise to the popular name of what to-day is the square called *Plaza de Pío XII*. This promenade (the *Borne*) was provided with four large oil lamps, which, in 1859, on the appearance of the first gas works in Majorca, were substituted by new gas-lighting. Almost simultaneously the boulevard called *La Rambla* was built, also above the disappeared river-bed. The *Rambla* was

←   Palma. The city from Maritime promenade.

←   Palma. Vía Roma (once La Rambla).

provided with a fountain also, at its northern end. This fountain, much altered, still exists. In 1852 the reform of the upper part of the city was begun, with the opening of the street called *Calle de Colón*, and work on the square to be called *Plaza Mayor* was commenced. In 1875 the first railway line *Palma-Inca* was inaugurated.

The 20th century, up to now, has been for the city an epoch of splendour of which nobody could ever have thought. In its early part the great expansion began. In 1902 the first electric power station was built and the Gran Hotel was opened, this being the first of the series of hotels which were to culminate in the splendid hotel industry of to-day. In 1911 the service of fast steamers which make the crossing Palma-Barcelona in eight hours was inaugurated. In 1916 came the electric tramways which connected the centre of the city with the suburbs and in the same year Hedilla make for the first time the crossing Barcelona-Palma by air. In 1931 comes the esplanade of *Santa Catalina (Se Faxina)*, which is to-day the square called *Crucero "Baleares"*. Then comes the "James the First" school, and, by virtue of a special law, the historic Castle of *Bellver* is handed over to the city. Between the years '50 and '60 come the transformations and alterations in the boulevards ("paseos"), the avenue called *Avenida de Jaime III* and the gardens of *S'Hort del Rei*, and the restoration of the Arab arch of the old city wall, the new market hall, the marine promenade called Paseo Marítimo, the great outer port, the airport, one of the busiest of Europe, and so on... In this century so far the city's population has quadrupled. With the enormous affluence of holidaymakers ("turistas") and going forward always on its own private initiative, Palma has situated itself among the first cities of the Mediterranean. (J. LLABRES BERNAL.)

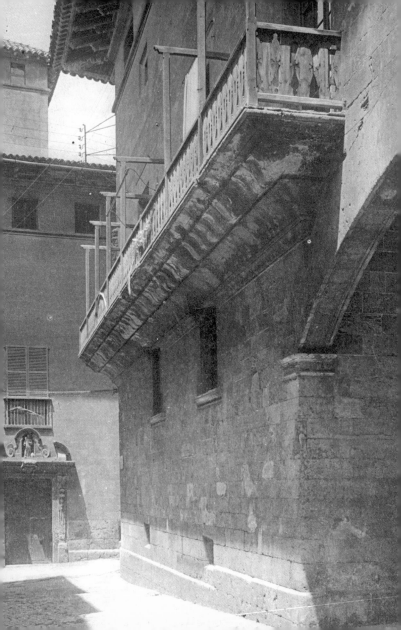

Courtyard in *La Concepción* street.

II.—PALMA AS A CITY OF THE PAST

ALMUDAINA ARCH AND ARAB BATHS. — Those are the only monuments left from the early Arab town, before 1229, the year in which the city was stormed by the Christians under King James I, the Conqueror.

The Almudaina Arch is situated in the street of the same name and it was one of the gates of the ramparts in the neighbourhood of the royal palace.

The Arab baths stand at 13 Calle Serra (Portella quarter) on the ground floor close to a picturesque garden and are privately owned. The vault is supported by twelve columns joined with horse-shoe-shaped arches in a small square room covered over with a small cupola. They are in good state of preservation.

The arch of *S'Hort del Rei* also Arabian is moulded in the wall which at that time was the "RONDA" (a clear space between a town and its walls) of *La Almudaina* palace, which has been restored. It is said that under this arch passed the vessels which carried the Wali who, during many centuries, ruled this island and had his residence in this palace.

← Palace of *Condé Formiguera*.

CASA MARQUES DE VIVOT COURTYARD.

Porch in *La Portella* street.

Entrance to Justice Palace

GOTHIC MONUMENTS (XIII to XV centuries). Noteworthy are the Cathedral, *La Lonja, San Francisco,* the *Almudaina* palace, the crypt of *San Lorenzo,* the churches of *Santa Eulalia, Santa Cruz, San Jaime* and *Santa Margarita,* the doorways of *San Nicolás,* the bell-tower, and doorway of *San Miguel,* the stairway of the *Casa Oleo,* the façade and refectory of the Convent of the Conception, the *coronelles* windows of the *Weyler* and *Montenegro* houses and *Alfarería* street. On the outskirts are the ancient walls of *Bellver* Castle and the *Pelaires* tower. All of these so closely linked with the history of the Kingdom of Majorca, will be fully dealt with under their respective headings.

Religious paintings of this time deserve as much attention as the master pieces of architecture mentioned before. The best examples of this art can be found in the Diocesan museum, the retable of *Saint George* by *Pere Nisart* is a true master piece, and in the Museum of the Cathedral. Other outstanding retables are those of the churches of *Montesión* and *Santa Eulalia,* in *Palma;* the retable of *Castellitx (Algaida)* and the retable of *Biniforam,* now belonging to March's private collection.

The most important sculptures of the island are: the sepulchre of Ramón Llull in *San Francisco* Church, the sepulchres of Bishop Ramón de Torrella and Bishop Galiana, both in the Cathedral, the statue of the Virgin of *La Grada*, also in the Cathedral. In the church of the city hospital there are two beautiful statues, the Virgin of *La Neu* and the Virgin of *Carmen*. In *San Miguel* Church there is the Virgin of *La Salut*, and in *San Jaime* Church *El Cristo del Santo Sepulcro* (The Christ of the Holy Sepulchre).

In the interior of the island, there are: The Virgin of *Lluch* and The Virgin of *Salvador (Artá);* the Processional Cross of *Porreras* and the retable in alabaster of *San Salvador (Felanitx).*

THE CATHEDRAL. — In September 1229, when the expedition under King James I was off Majorca a fierce gale raged and the King then vowed to erect a temple dedicated to the Virgin Mary should his enterprise succeed. He kept his promise and gave for this purpose the ground of seven houses out of the twenty which were his share of the *Almudaina*. The conquest was over and although the building was not to be completed until 1601; the High Altar was consecrated on October 1st 1346.

The cathedral is a Gothic building of great size. It covers an area of 7.000 square meters and is 121 meters long and 55 meters wide. Its plan is of the Roman style with a special apse for each of the three naves. The chief one is 20 meters wide and 75 meters long. It is prolonged to form the Royal Chapel. The aisles have the same length and are 10 meters wide. Thus there is formed a vault of stone with an area of 4.000 square meters, supported at a height of 45 meters by lofty octagonal columns about 1,25 meters in diameter. In 1903 under the superintendance of Architect Gaudí the choir was moved from the centre of the cathedral to the Royal Chapel thus giving the building its true liturgical meaning.

To behold the true grandeur of the Cathedral, the visitor should stand in the main entrace looking toward the High altar. From this spot its colossal size can best be valued.

Simplicity is its chief feature and although its ornaments are not equal to the magnificence of the building itself it has many a detail worth seeing — the tomb of Bishop Galiana in the Crown Chapel (15th century), wooden choirstalls dating from the period of transition between Gothic and Renaissance: the two pulpits, especially the left one with its remarkable reliefs and the gate of the old choir, are good speciments of the Renaissance style: the Chapter House with its Baroque gate and its small 18th century cloister. Inside the choir, forming another apse stands Holy Trinity chapel in whose wall are the Mausoleums of the Kings of Majorca James II and James III by sculptor Marés.

PALMA MAP

1. Cathedral.
2. *Almudaina* Palace.
3. *La Lonja* (museum, ancient trade exchange).
4. *Consulado del Mar.* Sea Consulate.
5. Bishop's Palace.
6. St. Peter & Bernard's.
7. *Almudaina* Arch.
8. Arabian Baths.
9. *Círculo Mallorquín.*
10. Town Hall.
11. *El Consell de Mallorca*
12. St. Francis's church.
13. St. Eulalia's.
14. St. Michael's.
15. St. Nicholas's.
16. St. James's.
17. St. Cross's.
18. Montesion's.
19. Perpetual Succour's.
20. St. Anthony's.
21. St. Clara's Convent.
22. Convent of the Conception.
23. St. Magdalena's Convent.
24. Olivar market square.
25. Civil Hospital.
26. Misericordia Asylum.
27. Marqués del Palmer's mansion.
28. Oleo's Palace.
29. Truyols's Palace.
30. Oleza's Palace.
31. Marqués de Vivot's Palace.
32. Verí's Palace.
33. Puigdorfila's Palace.
34. Marqués de Solleric's Palace.
35. Marcel's Palace.
36. March's Palace.
37. Palacio de Justicia.
38. Local Tourist Board.
39. Post & Telegraph Office.
40. Governor's House & Police.
41. Telephone Office.
42. Transmediterranean Company.
43. Nautical Club.
44. Sea Promenade.
45. Institute (Grammar School).
46. Railway Station.
47. Railway Station to Sóller.
48. Customs.

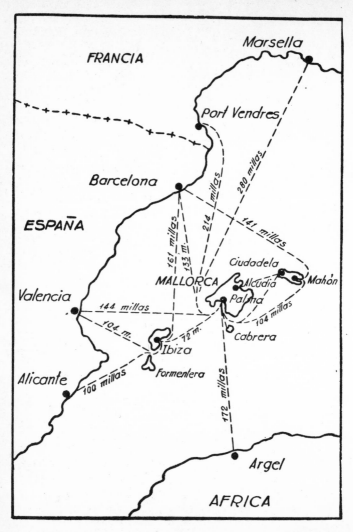

GEOGRAPHICAL POSITION OF MAJORCA
IN THE EASTERN MEDITERRANEAN

CASA OLEZA COURTYARD

Cloister of *San Antonio* (*San Miguel* street).

Also displayed are some remarkable paintings — a St. Sebastian a tryptisch of St. Eulalia, a great Gothic Altar Screen, a Renaissance picture, relics, jewels and objects for religious services. It possesses works of art of very great value — a magnificent shrine, a reliquiary, an ivory Christ, the seat used by Charles V when he came to Majorca, two magnificent seven-armed candelabras of silver and an outstanding collection of tapestries. All these works form a remarkable collection which are on display to visitors in the sacristy every day.

Outside the main façade, reconstructed in the middle of the 19th century, retains its "fantaisiste" main entrance. The main towers are 62 meters high. On the southern façade which faces the sea, the *Mirador* gate, a magnificent Gothic specimen worth seeing and at the tympanum a Lord's Supper carved by the Majorcan Sculptor Sagrera. The other façade the northern one, faces the city and displays the *Almoina* gate. On this side we find the old bell-tower. It is not yet completed although its construction was begun first. From the top of this tower a magnificent view of the harbour and the city is obtained. This tower has nine bells and one of them. N'Eloi, weighs 5.700 kgs. and is 2 meters in diameter.

Church of *Santa Catalina de Sena*.

Gardens of *S'Hort del Rei*.

Casa Morell façade.

Casa Morell courtyard.

Interiors of Morell Palace.

LA LONJA (OLD TRADE EXCHANGE) & THE SEA CONSULATE. — Both neighbouring buildings stand on *Paseo Sagrera* facing the sea. Between both is a small garden and by the promenade, re-erected after the dismantling of the ramparts, the XVII century Port Gate of the old walls through which people entered the city coming from the port.

The conquest over, James I gave the site on which to erect this building, although the edifice itselft was not to be constructed until the middle of the 15th century, under the supervision of the great Majorcan architect, Guillermo Sagrera. While admiring it, we conjure up the wealth and strength of Majorca in the middle ages, a civic building unique of its kind. It covers an area 40 meters long and 28 meters wide and the corners are crowned with 4 octagonal turrets. These are easily reached and from them we get a magnificent panorama of port and city. The main gates, remarkable on account of its sculptures; has glazed windows and such architectural features as gargoyles and cornices. The interior is a hall whose vaulted roof is supported by six wreathed columns, which on reaching ceiling level stretch forth in the shape of a mineboughed palm tree.

The Sea Consulate is the old seat of the Trading Courts and is remarkable on account of its façade overlooking the port, a renaissance gallery of five arches and a magnificent panelled ceiling. Behind it, stands a tiny Oratory whose façade on the *Lonja* side dates back to the period of Gothic decadence.

EPISCOPAL PALACE AND DIOCESAN MUSEUM. — It rises in line with the cathedral facing the sea. It is a building of imposing proportions, with a central court yard and gardens. It contains a gallery of paintings with the portraits of all the bishops of the past history of Majorca. The Diocesan Museum occupies part of the ground floor, which in older times were the bishop's quarters with the chapelle of St. Paul of the XIV and XV centuries. The entrance is from the square, with a doorway of the same period. The museum contains various valuable altar screens and other gothic objects.

Church of *San Francisco* façade. →

City Hall.

ST. FRANCIS CONVENT.

ST. FRANCIS CONVENT. — The whole building is one of the architectural jewels of the city. The 14th century Gothic church has a single nave 75 meters long, 17 meters wide and 25 meters high. Under the choir we find the tomb of the Majorcan poligraph and learned philosopher, missionary and martyr, Raymond Llull. The style of the tomb is late Gothic.

The 17th century façade belongs to the Baroque and whimsical styles and a beautiful main entrance. The 13th and 14th century Gothic cloister is a gem of that period architecture. It is remarkable too on account of its size which is far greater than the typical of that time. On the walls are a number of memorial tablets. The building itself embraces four galleries and a well laid-out garden with, in the middle, a well dating back to 1652. This building is unique of its kind and is classified as a National Monument. The residence of the Franciscan monks is also worth visiting. A room with a magnificent panelled ceiling, a Gothic altar screen and many other works amounting in all to a small museum, are found here. Also worth seeing are the typically Majorcan choir and sacristy.

Palma. Maritime promenade. →

Almond trees in bloom. →

Courtyard in *San Roque* - Courtyard in San Pedro & San Bernardo street.

ALMUDAINA PALACE. — On a site commanding the entrance to the city, facing the sea and in line with the Cathedral, stands the palace. It embraces an area of 20.000 square meters. This in the ancient Palace of the Moorish Kings. It was rebuilt in the 12th and 14th centuries by the Kings of Majorca who established their abode there, after the conquest. Later on, it belonged to the Kings of Aragon and then to the Kings of Spain. Since then it has been part of the Royal demesne. Restored of late, it is now the seat of the Military Command, of the Courts of Justice and the Archives. The most important features of this great building are — besides the façade overlooking the sea with its two towers as a frame for the Gothic gallery — the large central courtyard and St. Anne's Chapel, which we find on entering the main gateway (opposite the Cathedral). The gate of the chapel is of Roman Style. Inside the chapel itself is a 12th century screen and some interesting architectural details.

← Beach of *Santa Ponsa*.

← Diocesan Museum. *San Jorge* de Nisart (XV century).

PORTELLA QUARTER & ARAB BATHS. — Further along the waterfront, this typical quarter stands on the ancient walls just below the Episcopal Palace. On account of the stately mansions all around — those of the España family, the Marqués de la Torre, *Formiguera* and *Desbrull* — it is a most impressive quarter. A visit to this secluded and isolated district is always interesting and is most necessary for sightseers to the city. Its centre is Portella Street and it consists of a dozen or so quiet, narrow, steep winding lanes branching from the first.

TOWN HALL. — Rising from *Cort* Square, vital trade centre of the city, it presents a pure Renaissance 17th century façade. From this, the carved eaves to form a notable work on account of both richness and size. The inside of the building is modern and nothing need to be said of either its staircase or the Council Chamber. It has some interesting works among them a painting by Van Dick representing St. Sebastian and an old strong box.

THE SEA WALLS. — In the past, Palma was a walled city. The last walls to be built were after the design of the Italian engineer Fratin, they were started in 1562. Of all this military work nothing remains but the section overlooking the sea that in spite of the many mutilations it has endured, is still in state of good repair, as also are the four remaining bastions, out of the thirteen that originally formed the compound. Two of the old doorways *La Portella* and *La Calatrava*, out of the nine that existed can also be seen.

Courtyard in *El Sol* street   Courtyard in *General Goded* street.

Casal Balaguer courtyard.

67

Casal Balaguer

Zavellá street.

CHURCHES. — Churches, convents, monasteries and oratories are in such number that we will only list the most important ones.

Church of St. Eulalia: Built in the 13th and 14th centuries. Consists of three naves supported by 18 columns and covers an area 57 meters long and 27 meters wide. Restored of late, its façade has been reconstructed and the building now has a spire. The side façades are Gothic. Inside are some interesting paintings especially a Gothic altar screen in the first chapel from the right. The high altar is Roccoco. Apart from the Cathedral it is the largest and the most important church in *Palma.*

Church of the Sacred Cross: It is in the 15th and 16th century Gothic styles. It has one nave and there are some features of recent construction. St. Lawrence's crypt is remarkable. As far as Gothic is concerned it is the oldest example of the style in the city. It is very small, situated under the High Altar and the entrance is in the street of same name.

Church of St. James: It is of good proportions and displays but a single nave. It was begun in the 14th century and completed in the 19th. It was founded by the Kings of Majorca.

68

Majorcan Manorial House bedroom. →

Church of St. Michael: Situated on the site where the ancient Mosque stood, it was consecrated on the very day of the Conquest. The present church is not very old. Inside can be seen the image of the Virgin of Health, a superb piece which King James carried on board his ship and deposited here on entering the city.

The Church of St. Margaret: This ancient convent is situated at the end of *San Miguel* street. It was founded in the 14th century by the king Jaime II. Once, used as a warehouse, now restored and declared national monument.

Church of St. Nicholas: It dates from the 14th and 15th centuries. Although now reconstructed, its main door dates from that period.

St. Peter & St. Bernard is a small oratory with "fantaisiste" façade. Here is to be found the asylum or hospital for poor and disabled priests. Its courtyard is remarkable and one of the most representative in the city.

Montesión is a centre of secondary education. It has been very well restored by the Jesuits. The Baroque entrance to the church itself is worthy of note on account of its originality. It contains the tomb of St. *Alonso Rodríguez* together with a very remarkable altar screen.

Church of El Socorro. A 15th century building, it is chiefly remarkable on account of its spire and St. Nicholas Chapel with its richly ornamented cupola.

Former convent of St. Anthony in *St. Miguel* Street. The church, elliptical in shape, is small and the Florentine style dominates. A fine piece of work of the late XVIII century, it is the only one in *Palma* displaying fresco paintings. To have it always closed is regrettable. In order to visit it, one should apply at the vestry of *San Miguel* church almost opposite.

Saint Clair convent: A typical feature of the town because of the entrance patio. The humble church completes the ensemble.

Convent of Saint Magdalen (23). — A finely balanced building with high cupola. Although of very old foundation the construction is of XVIII century. The incorrupt body of Santa Catalina Tomás is kept here in an urn. The Majorcan saint was a religious nun of this convent in the XVI century.

Convent of the Conception. It was formerly the stately mansion of the Zaforteza family. The façade is chiefly remarkable for her gothic panes *(finestres coronellas)* recently restored and restituted to the original construction of XIV century. In the cloister are several gothic paintings, a baroque patio and a remarkable refectory of XV century.

Casa Veri courtyard.

COURTYARD & STATELY MANSIONS. — The strong trade bonds linking Majorca and the Italian states in the 15-17-18th centuries caused the new artistic trends of the Italian Renaissance to make a definite impression on the Majorcan style of building. The island building style is an adaptation of the Italian, a large open central patio of square or rectangular shape in the corners of which are columns and the arches they support, and in the inner part —or one of the corners— the large staircase.

The façade is simple, with a semi-circular arch above the gateway. Before the 17th century these houses had a terrace with pergola which later on was turned into a large garret.

On the ground floor there are large halls *(entradas)* with their ceilings made first of many coloured woods and later on panelled in red pine *(llenyam vermell)* and large yards where coaches were kept. An upper floor surmounted by an attic or another storey completes the building. In many cases the staircase finishes up in a gallery.

In spite of considerable Italian influence all of them retain the usual features of the typical Majorcan construction; Ramis de Ayreflor remarks on this. "These are rather transformations than new designs, consisting in new windows on the first storey and attic and in enlargements of courtyards and gateways. But these transformations are always based on the Gothic which does not disappear here, giving, way as it does to the "platerescô" style — profuse decoration of flowers and leaves — and later to the Baroque. Such embellishments as these, increase the beauty of the city.

Inside, the first floor is divided into large and lofty salons, all of them communicating so that on important occasions they can be turned into one large room. The style of decoration is simple but rich — panelled in red pine, the walls are hung with damask and sumptuous curtains and tapestries.

Typical furniture is: chair upholstered in leather or velvet with Renaissance nailed seats; trunks and coffers of the Gothic, Floral and Baroque styles and the small arches typical of the country. Bedrooms have four-poster beds with damask curtains and altar screens of great value. The number of works of art (paintings, sculptures, potery, etc.) which remains in these stately mansions is — in spite of losses — of incalculable value.

A straightforward description, or even enumeration, of all these houses would require so much space that only the most important ones will be named. In the lower part of the city are *Casa Berga* (Map no. 37), Saint Catherine Thomas Square

---

INCREASE OF TOURIST IN MAJORCA, TOTAL NUMBER OF PASSENGERS, ENTERING AND LEAVING PALMA; BY SEA AND BY AIR

1959	1.007.202 passengers
1960	1.118.612 passengers
1961	1.400.351 passengers
1962	1.599.501 passengers
1963	1.765.279 passengers
1964	2.150.946 passengers
1965	2.603.649 passengers
1966	2.992.080 passengers
1967	3.327.929 passengers
1968	3.769.581 passengers
1969	4.698.237 passengers
1970	5.573.201 passengers
1971	6.888.845 passengers
1972	7.773.568 passengers
1973	7.958.545 passengers
1974	7.578.284 passengers
1975	7.866.108 passengers
1976	7.560.707 passengers
1977	8.098.909 passengers
1978	9.026.144 passengers
1979	9.078.892 passengers
1980	8.413.460 passengers

Manorial House Hall.

with its courtyard and balcony running the whole length of the façade: *Casa Puigdorfila* (33) at number 10 in the street of the same name; *Casa Verí* (32), at 16 *Verí* Street; *Casa del Marqués de Solleric* (34) San Cayetano Street, opposite the church and with a façace overlooking the *Borne* promenade; *Casa del Marqués de Casa Ferrandell*, 21 San Jaime Street; *Casa Marcel* (35), 7 San Juan Street; *Casa Marqués*, 51 Apuntadores Street and *Casa Villalonga*, 29 Gloria Street.

In the higher part of the city are *Casa Marqués del Palmer* (27), 17 Sol Street, with its magnificent façade of purest Renaissance; *Casa Marqués de Vivot* (31), with a superb staircase of Baroque style and gallery, Zavellá Street; *Casa Oleza* (30), 33 Morey Street (beautiful gallery windows and well in courtyard). In the *Portella* quarter the *Casa* (houses) of *Formiguera*; at no. 8. Almudaina Street stands *Casa Oleo* (28) still retaining its Gothic staircase, other houses of note are those of the *Marqués de la Torre*, *España*, *Desbrull*, etc. In Almudaina Street at no. 11 is *Casa Truyols* and just close by *Casa Villalonga* remarkable on account of its front windows.

Apart from the stately town —houses of Mallorca there are also the country houses. If the first are magnificent and beautiful, even more magnificent are the latter with their fine gardens and fountains. They are nothing less than palaces and they will be mentioned when island excursions are dealt with.

Manorial House Hall.

In every palace in the old Town there lived an aristocratic family and many times the street where it is situated has the family name which never is changed although the manor house which gave the name to the street has disappeared. In front of the house there was a little square to make easy the turning of the coaches.

All these families have, besides the house in *Palma* a country one. If the first one is large and beautiful the second is even larger with its gardens and fountains, real palaces which will be described during the excursions. Besides other properties each family had a preferred residence whose name was the same as the family preceded by Son, which means property of, equivalent to the French "Chez". All the houses lay on the heights round the town and not far from it, about 10-20-25 kms., and always distant from the sea. They are from the 16th and 17th centuries and usually very well preserved. The owner always lives on the first floor where the distribution is the same and the furniture as magnificent as in the palace in *Palma* but with bigger interior court "clastre", and galleries towards the garden. The places most frequented are: *Puigpuñent, Esporlas, Valldemosa, Buñola, Santa María, Alaró*, etc. The custom is to stay in town during summer and winter and spend spring and autumn in the country. The favorite entertainment is then to hunt.

74

Casa Colom courtyard · Zanglada street.

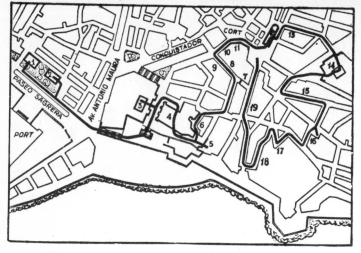

A BRIEF VISIT TO THE OLD CITY (The numbers refer to the Sketch).

Those who wishes to know the monuments of Palma should assign himself at least two whole days in order to devote the required time to appreciate each one of them.

However, a visitor may have to reckon on an afternoon or morning time only or perhaps even a few hours. To enable him to get a general idea, a sort of summing up, of the old city features, we suggest this short route:

Starting from the town entrance proceed along the *Sagrera* Promenade where rise the Sea Consulate (1) and the Lonja (2); between the two monuments you can see the old to the City of Palma, previously located at the entrance of Antonio Maura street on along the town walls, on the left you can see the new *Parque de Mar* recently built, leaving the *Almudaina* Palace on your left walk up the steps leading to the Mirador. You can visit the courtyard of *Almudaina* Palace (3), then the Cathedral (4) and the Episcopal Palace (5) following the San Bernardo street you enter the courtyard of the oratory. Now pass along through San Pedro Nolasco Street where the arch of this name is to be found (7). Keeping to Zanglada Street on the left will lead you to *Almudaina*, to the left you shall see the windows of *Casa Villalonga* and *Truyol* (8) on the right, and on the left *Casa Oleo* (9). On entering Palacio Street (*Palau Reial* Street) (10) is the *Consell de Mallorca Palace* on the right and in Cort Square you walk by the Town Hall (11). From there, in the centre of the city, continue through *Cadenas* Street and St. Eulalia Square where you can visit the Church (12); then passing behind the Church you come to Zavellá Street where you can visit the house of the Marquis of *Vivot* (13). Continuing along through the same street (Zavella Street) you reach the front of St. Francis Church (14) where you can enter in order to visit the tomb of Raymond Llull and specially the cloister (entrance from St. Francis Square). Leaving this square and walking into Arquitecto Reynés street, you find in the left, Padre Nadal Street and turning to the left *Sol* Street and at no. 17 the façade of *Casa Marqués del Palmer* (15).

Going down *Sol* Street you find on the right a narrow side street, *Crianza* Street, which leads you to *Montesión* square (16). Here you can see the great doorway (18). Then you continue by *Viento* Street, alongside the church, as far as St. Alonso Street. Walk this street down to the right side street leading to the courtyard of *Santa Clara* Convent (17). On along the street of the same name you come to *Serra* Street on the left, where you can visit the Arab Baths (18). Continue by *Formiguera* and *Portella* Street, passing as you do so, the façades and courtyards of many fine mansions. Next comes *Morey* Street with *Casa Oleza* (19) on the right. Visit its courtyard. Then proceed to *Cort* Square and that is the end of a quick excursion through the city.

This itinerary as well as the following is more convenient to go on foot, each of them takes about two hours. Nevertheless horse carriages can be hired, which are suitable to travel through the streets of the old town.

Way up to the Cathedral.

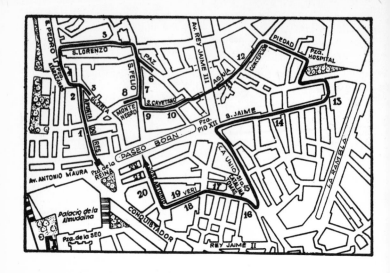

SECOND ITINERARY TO VISIT THE TOWN. — For the persons having a spare morning or afternoon and wishing to visit the western part of the town, greatly modernized, we suggest this second itinerary.

Starting from *La Reina* square, we begin our tour by *Apuntadores* street, where on the left side near. *St. Juan* street, we can find *Marcel's* Mansions (1) with its courtyard and further on Marques' Mansions (2) with its spacious entrance and its beautiful staircase. At the end of this street we can turn to *La Gloria* street where, at number 25, we can see a baroque window (3). Turning to the left we cross *Atarazanas* square in the centre of which there is a statue of *Jaume Ferrer*, a great Majorcan navigator of Middle Ages. Leaving this square we take *St. Pedro* street, and we turn to the right by *St. Lorenzo* street, where, on the left side, there is a crypt of the same name, a monument of the XII century (5). At the end of this street, in *La Paz* square, we can admire *Weyler's* Mansion with its gothic arched windows (6).

Going down this square, we take *St. Felio* street on the left side of which there is *Bellot's* Mansion with its beautiful entrance (7). Turning to the right, by *Montenegro* street, we can see the Palace of the same name, with its façade, with its coat of arms and gothic window (8). Going back we take *St. Caye-*

78

tano street; on the right side of this street there is the oratory of *St. Felio* (9), a little further on in the same street, we can see an XVIII century courtyard, in *Morell's* Mansion (10) one of the most interesting in the city. Following the same direction we cross *Jaime III* Avenue, a new avenue with its modern buildings, a magnificent example of the progress of *Palma* in the last few years. Taking *Agua* street we can see the typical fountain of the *Sepulcro* (11) an further on, on the left side, the façade of the convent of *La Concepción* (12), with its primitive gothic windows.

We turn to the right by *La Piedad* street and we reach *Hospital* square, where there is a hospital formerly built in the XV century and nowadays modernized. From this place we take *Sta. Magdalena* street with the church of the same name, built in the XVIII century (13), where *Sta. Catalina Tomás*, a Majorcan saint is buried. From this point we take *San Jaime* street, on the left of which we can see the church of the same name (14), at both sides of this street there are several mansions, which are named after the families *(Orlandis, Torrella, Roses, Ferrandell, San Simón, Ribas, Marqués del Reguer, Armengol*, etc.), all these mansions with beautiful courtyards and façades.

At the bottom of this street there is the modern square of *Pío XII* and in its centre the fountain of *Las Tortugas*. Without crossing this square and following on the left, there is *La Unió* street, we come to *St. Catalina* square, with is gardens; in the center is the statue of *Antonio Maura* (15), a great Spanish politician of the beginning of this century. In the same square there is the old *Berga's* Mansion (16) that has recently been transformed into the new Court of Justice; in the same square there is *St. Nicolás* church (17).

Without changing our direction, we take *Verí* street, where at number 7 (18) we can admire a beautiful baroque window and the courtyard of *Verí's* mansion (19), built during the Renaissance. At the end of this street is *La Constitució* Avenue with its modern buildings, the Central Post Office (20), the residence of the governor (21) among them and the telephone exchange. At the end of this avenue there is the tradicional *Borne*, where we began our 2nd. tour, formerly the bank of "La Riera" when this river crossed the town, later turned into a square where tournaments where celebrated, and since a century is the favourite walk of the local people. That ends the tour of the lower town in the most interesting part.

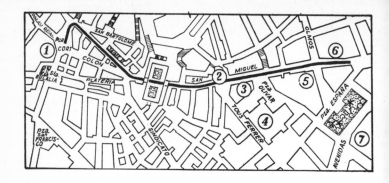

THIRD ITINERARY TO VISIT THE TOWN.—Let us begin at *Cort* Square, the classic centre of a traditional city. Here is the Town Hall (1) with its XVI century façade, clock and tower, with her popular bell *En Figuera*, that for so many years governs the life of the city, sometimes in the form of an alarm as in the case of fire and keeping the time. Nowadays this is past history since the creation of a firehouse and radios in all the homes.

The first part of our tour will be through the business section. Beginning at *Jaime II* street, without motor traffic and with all kind of business shops. At the end of this street we take to the left *Sindicato* street, parallel, to cross over to *Plaza Mayor* with entrance to *San Miguel* street. These two narrow streets were always commercial and used to be named after their respective guilds. *Jaime II* was formerly known as the street of the *bastaxos* (porter in the street) and *Sindicato* as *Sa Capelleria* (hats) but they have lost their names as small shops turned into big stores.

The church of *San Miguel* (2) is the first of four in this street, all very interesting. It is the oldest in the city. Here was once an Arab mosque that was consacrated christian the day of the conquest. Her façade, porch and belfry are gothic.

The church of *San Antonio* (3) is an interesting example of the XVIII century with its dome decorated with frescos, and small cloister, both of elliptic shape. It is regrettable that it is always closed. It only opens for the feast of the Saint on January 17th, in which day is celebrated before the church the traditional beneide (blessing) of the cavalries, at one time of supreme height, and nowaday fading more and more with the introduction of motor vehicles.

Then we come to the *Olivar* square (4) and market place where a popular commercial district has developed as an annex. This area is lively at any time of the day.

80

Beach of *Magalluf*. →
Beach of Palma. *Ca'n Pastilla*. →

The church of *Santa Catalina de Sena* (5) an XVIII century building and the only thing left from the old convent that was demolished and sold as lots over which big dwellings with commercial galleries have been built. The church was the only thing saved from the old convent thanks to being declared national monument.

Santa Margarita (6), monument of the XIV century, served for more than a century as a warehouse. Now it has been modernly restored and declared a national monument. Today the Military Hospital occupies the old ground of the convent.

And we reach the end of *San Miguel* street, the longest of the old city, which leads to the boulevards of the new section, which are the main thoroughfare. They have been built where the old walls used to be, which were demolished at the begining of this century. In this junction was the old door of Bab al Kofor, a remainder of the old Arab wall which was demolished in 1912. On December 31, 1228 and through this door, King *Jaime I* entered triumphant in front of his army and conquered the city after breaking through the walls.

Church of Santa Margarita.

← Beach of Palma. *El Arenal.*

← Palma. *Pelaires* Tower.

The giants of the city.

Font del Sepulcre (La Concepción street)

Typical balcony (La Misión street).

III. — PALMA, TYPICAL CITY

The traditional typicalness is gradually disappearing in all the villages and towns, in the latter more quickly. In the first years of this century the servant girls in the city came from the villages and they all wore the typical peasant dress. The great expansion of the city, which began in 1902 with the walls down has meant the disappearance of many typical corners, and if we add the series of demolitions carried out with the object of internal improvements and the creation of new commercial thoroughfares, as well as constructions on new sites, we see that the city is in a continuous process of modernisation, it has changed and goes on changing its aspect.

Nevertheless in spite of so much development that have parted with so much of the old, we still have many corners, streets, squares and even buildings which still retain their original character, mainly in the outer suburbs facing the sea, *La Cala-trava* to the East and *El Puig de Sant Pere* to the West. We might also mention the *El Jonquet* quarter, with its old wind-mills, now converted into night-clubs. The windmills of the eastern area have disappeared completely. Some towers of what were flour-making mills still exist on the *Son Rapinya* road, now called *Calle de la Industria*. Outside the city and almost adjoining the walls existed a great ring of popular eating-houses, all of which have now disappeared because of the city's typical corners, also in the process of disappearing, it is still a source of inspiration for the artists whose works may be admired at the exhibitions which are held in the art galleries of the city.

Some festivals and traditional customs also still remain. The most noteworthy are those of Holy week, with its processions, the most impressive being that of Holy Thursday which starts at nightfall from the Hospital Church and passes through the main streets of the town, watched by an immense crowd of people. In it participate more than 30 confraternities, with their monumental set-pieces, authentic works of art, and more than 2.000 penitents. On the night of Good Friday is celebrated the Holy Sepulture. The procession starts from the Cathedral and in profound silence traverses the upper city. Similarly the Feast of *Corpus Christi* still exist. The procession starts at dusk from the Cathedral, and troops line the road. There is a great ani-mation in the streets on the day of the festival.

Tamborés de la Sala (City Council's Durum Band).

The traditional festivities organised by the Town Hall and attended by the corporation are those of the 3rd of July at the church of San Francisco in honour of the beatified *Ramón Llull*, the glory of medieval Majorcan letters; that of the 28th of July at *Santa Magdalena* in honour of Saint *Catalina Tomás*, nun of this convent in the sixteenth century; and that of the 31st December, the most solemn of all, to commemorate the entry into the city of King James the First on wresting it from the Arabs, who had occupied it during four centuries. The façade of the Town Hall is adorned and the portrait of the Conqueror King presides it. The retinue comes out of the Town Hall and places the royal standard in the centre of the square, *Plaza de Cort*. The City Mounted Police initiate the march, followed by the *"tambores de la sala"* (drummers), the *"ministrils"*, the mace-bearers and state guards, the Municipal Government in full force and, closing the procession, the Municipal Band. The procession proceeds to the Cathedral, where a great religious act is celebrated, with the collaboration of the authorities. This concluded, the procession returns to the Town Hall by the same route, bearing the royal standard. A company of Infantry with banner, band and music render the royal honours, firing the regulation volley on the hoisting and retiring of the royal standard.

View of *Puig de Sant Pere* quarter.

IV.—PALMA'S MODERN CITY

The scenary, monuments, the typical villages and towns powerfully appealed to our 19th century visitor. Most of them were artists and writers eager to discover ways of life unknown to them.

Trully, nowadays there does still exist a holidaymaker seeking relaxation in the country or on a beach, but the present day tourist prefers ready made holidays. He is interested in town life because of the comfort, entertainments and facilities it affords.

All the latter can be found in *Palma*, a city which visitors have so much contributed to adapt to a modern life. In the summer it is easy to undertake an excursion or a trip to a beach from the town or in winter whenever we miss the so called ideal climate, a cliche we have so much overused, it is easy to find in any café, bar or place of entertainment the advantages of a nice central-heating system.

HARBOUR AND MARITIME AREA OF THE TOWN

The nucleos of the town borders the sea with a front of 6 kms. it extends from *Pelaires* to the *Portitxol*. It consists of a promenade continued by a thoroughfare of double road of three runways each. The first strecht of this promenade has the big hotels and the tall modern buildings. On the second strecht one finds the principal historical monuments of the town (*Consulado del Mar, Lonja, La Almudaina* palace, and the old town walls) the third strecht, in contrast with the two others is an old suburb of the town, at present under development. There are some patches of green on this long promenade. The palm trees was imported during the arab domination from the IX to XIII centuries. Today is the main ornament of this promenade, we find them in long lines or grouped together in little gardens, enchanting its beauty and character. There are over 700 of them, some, very high. The large number of these trees are by itself a proof of the mild climate of the island.

(See the plan of this beautiful promenade.)

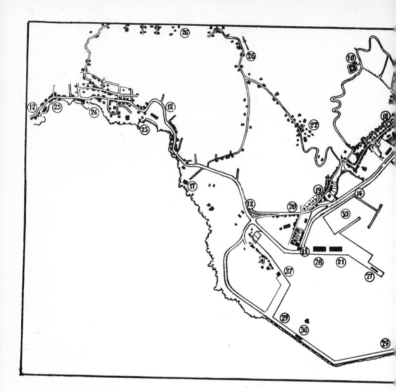

1. OLD TOWN WALLS.
2. EPISCOPAL PALACE - DIOCESAN MUSEUM.
3. CATHEDRAL.
4. *LA ALMUDAINA* PALACE & *S'HORT DEL REI* GARDENS.
5. *LA LONJA*.
6. *CONSULADO DEL MAR*.
7. *CLUB NAUTICO*.
8. TENNIS CLUB.
9. CUSTOMS HOUSE.
10. *BELLVER* CASTLE.
11. *PELAIRES* TOWER.
12. ROAD TO *ANDRAITX*.
13-14. DOCKS.
15. *C.ª TRANSMEDITERRANEA*. SPANISH REGULAR BOAT SERVICE.
16. MARITIME PROMENADE *GABRIEL ROCA*.
17. *MARIVENT*
18. *EL TERRENO*.
19. *CORP MARI*.
20. *PORTO PI*.

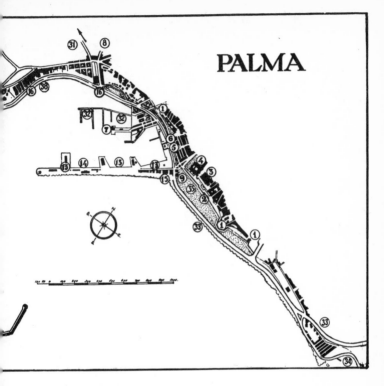

PALMA

Rey Jaime III Avenue.

The wealth of a region is best shown in the merits of the town it has been able to originate. In this respect *Palma* shelters 50 %· of the inhabitants of the whole island. Few towns have achived its progress in the past half century: its population 64.000 inh. in 1901 is up to 290.000 nowadays. In spite of this change its typical quarters and monuments have almost been kept intact and some have even improved.

The dismantling of the 17th century city walls began in 1902. They stifled the city and prevented any structure being built within 2 kms. on the outside. Nowadays, on the site of those walls there is a 5 km. long and, 40 m. wide avenue laid in zig zag from where start a large number of streets with modern buildings all this makes up the new town *(Ensanche)* which is three times the old town in area. The centre is *España* square (15.000 square feet), by the railways station. A statue of King James I, the city conqueror stands in the centre surrounded with gardens. On account of this expanding new town the old out districts have been integrated into the town which has rounded them up and forms one body with them. *El Terreno* district, once a summer resort, connected to the town by a mule drawn tramway, is now a privileged and selected summer and residential resort.

Principal Theatre.

Social and touristic life are centred in modern *Palma* on Promenade *Borne*, built around the middle of the 19th century where the main cafés, bars, restaurants, entertainments halls, clubs, travel agencies are located, making it a lively thoroughfare at any time.

By sitting at one of the café terraces, in the shade of one of the stout trees — a blessing in the summer — you can see the town life flowing. Here all social classes meet and mingle with a procession of people of every nationality speaking their various languages and wearing most varied apparels. Cars displaying, platenumbers from all the countries in the world, buses, taxicabs, crowded touring-coaches, motorcycles also make their way along.

The waiters can speak some foreign languages and altogether we have the atmosphere of a cosmopolitan town.

The *Borne* was subjected in 1956 to a most unfortunate and unpopular replanning. The stately promenade has been shortened and at both ends two squares have been laid, and so the beautiful trees once standing there have disappeared. The painful mutilation has not improved the town in any way. This traditional promenade is still the most popular in the town.

The *Borne* is linked to *Paseo de Sagrera* through *Avenida Antonio Maura*. The former promenade is called after the architect who built *La Lonja*. The promenade displays a double

91

La Reina Square.

row of palm trees and is situated on the site of the dismantled ramparts. The promenade is prolonged by *Paseo Marítimo* which goes round all along the sea up to *Son Armadams. El Terreno, Corp Marí* and *Porto Pi*, districts. On this promenade a number of splendid hotels and up to date dwellings as well as cafés and bars have been set up. All this can be regarded as a prolongation of the *Borne*. The town can boast of some other promenades such as *La Rambla*, inside the thown and the jetty walk located on the former jetty of the older harbour, about 1 km. long. It affords a magnificent view on one side of the shipping docks and quays and busy traffic, and on the other of the vast bay.

The older part respecting however the architectural treasures and monuments has been subjected to important replanning and so has been embellished. Let us mention the new market-place *Olivar* a model of its kind, the building which construction caused an old and destitute quarter to disappear and in its turn is *Plaza Mayor* (Main Square); where the old market was is now a beautiful square. All around the up-to-date market place stand modern and fine structures, bank and commercial firms buildings. Another important replanning has been going on around *Jaime III* thoroughfare. The latter lined with magnificent porticoed buildings connects in the higher part by *Jaime I* school building where the crowded quarter of *Santa Catalina* begins.

Gardens of *S'Hort del Rei*.

Among modern buildings we should mention March's palace, amounting to a fine arts museum, the provincial branch of the Treasury, the secondary school building, the Bank of Bilbao and the Bank Español de Crédito. Quite apart from all this we have the County Council Hall. We will remark the façace, a reminder of *La Lonja*, the staircase the entrance hall, the council chamber and the chairman's office. Here is, too, a remarkable library meant for superior learning on the ground-floor.

In a modern city we cannot fail to find a complete scale of entertainments and sports, dance halls, all the year round cinemas and theatres, bull ring, tennis courts, velodrome, football rings, swimmings pools. We should particularly mention, the Yacht Club, a model of its kind covering an area of over 40.000 square m. with over 800 pleasure craft where occasionally over 50 yatchs of all flags are moored. *El Círculo Mallorquín* a 100 years old club is also a model of its kind. It is situated in a selfowned building overlooking *Palau Reial* street and *Conquistador* street. A notable library, sumptuous rooms and a magnificent dance hall are the chief features of the club where society people usually meet.

Let us mention the great and up-to-date harbour now just about to be completed, with docks able to berth the biggest liners. The total length is 8 kms. out of which 4 make up by the maritime promenade connecting the commercial docks and

Monument to King James I

Monument to *Hondero Balear.*

Yacht Club.

Pío XII Square

Fountain in Vía Roma
(old Rambla promenade).

Mallorca promenade.

Maritime promenade Gabriel Roca.

passenger quays for mail and passengers ships to the liners quay and western jetty nearly 2 kms. long.

The large majority of the people of Majorca are catholics. However the protestant religion is practiced. The Anglican church has its seat in Núñez de Balboa street, *Son Armadams*, the Evangelical church is situated in 16 Murillo Street. Tel. 231.810. Services are held in Spanish, French, English, German and Dutch.

Her life as a capital is more active than any other city with a larger number of inhabitants. With 47.000 telephones, hundreds of touristic offices and over 500 modern coaches exclusively for excursions is relatively the second capital of Spain. About 20.000 men are presently working in the construction of new buildings. There are over 200.000 licensed vehicles being per capita the first province of Spain with such a number and if to this we add the number of national and foreign tourist vehicles you would understand the traffic problem and parking difficulties in the city.

The *Paseo Marítimo* has been the base of the deep transformation of modern *Palma*. The city should be grateful to a great Majorcan, the engineer Gabriel Roca who first conceived and carried into practice such a wonderful project. The maritime promenade was built on land gained to the ocean. It begins at the mouth of a torrent, *La Riera* that for centuries poured its

Beach of *Palma Nova*. →

Beach of *Paguera*. →

Maritime promenade.

Maritime promenade.

← Colonia de *Sant Jordi* (Harbour of *Campos*).

← *Valldemosa*.

Maritime promenade.

Pelaires Docks.

water into a corner of the harbour till it became a small swamp, closing it in part. The *Club Náutico*, one of the most important of the Mediterranean basin was built on one side of the mouth and at the other side the *Paseo Marítimo*. This worthless land turned into a beautiful boulevard and the plots that had no value are today the site of beautiful de luxe hotels. Such magnificent thoroughfare shortly became the busiest of the city and no sooner was it finished that it clearly became a necessity to double its width which now after the reform is over 40 m. and in some parts even twice as much. It has double line traffic with small gardens and parking facilities. At the seaside a beautiful yatch pier was built skirting all its extension. At the opposite side you will see a beautiful line of hotels, bars, restaurants, travel agencies, shops, etc.

No far away from the *Paseo Marítimo* you will find the Spanish Village. Surrounded by ramparts with its towers and merlons a reproduction built of the most characteristic and typical of Spain. About a hundred artistic and architectonic monuments of different styles and dating from different epochs has been selected and carefully reproduced. It is impossible now to give you a detail of them because of its complexity. Next to it was built the *Palacio de Congresos,* a monumental building which is devoted to international assemblies and meetings. As an annex to this palace a Roman Amphitheatre was built.

Another great realizations of modern *Palma* is the highway to the airport, which begins at the junction of the *Sagrera* promenade and the harbour road following on land gained to the ocean thus developing a new east maritime promenade. At *Ca'n Pastilla* (km. 7) it splits into two roads, one leading straight to the airport and the other skirting the *Playa de Palma* with its beautiful line of hotels and ending at *El Arenal*, having in all an extension of 13 kms.

An outstanding feature of the Season is *Palma* by night, mainly concentrated in two large seaside avenues. To the east, the five km. long beach *Playa de Palma* between *Ca'n Pastilla* and *El Arenal*. To the west, the 7 km. long sea front promenade, that starts at *Paseo Sagrera* continuing along *Paseo Marítimo, Cala Mayor* up to *Ca's Catalá*. Both avenues are populated by cars and crowds, and lined by an endless line of hotels, cafes, bars, night clubs, etc., brightly lit, and it is the life of the town during the summer months.

Marine Club *Porto Pi*.

Queen Elizabeth II at the Maritime station.

Boat Canberra (46.000 tons), leaving the port.

Maritime station for transatlantic liners.

International Airport of *Son Sanjuán*.

Highway to the airport.

V. — THE ENVIRONS OF THE TOWN

The old town is joined to the modern one, and this is connected to the surroundings by a bus service. The services most interesting for the visitors are those that start at *Pláza de la Reina* (end of *Borne* promenade) and go to *El Terreno, Porto Pi, Ca's Catalá* and *Génova,* and also to the beaches and resorts of the Western coast; *Illetas, Portals Nous* and *Palma Nova.* There is another service that starts at *Plaza de España,* stopping in *Pío XII,* and continues along *Jaime III* avenue to the *Andraitx* main road up to *Magalluf, Santa Ponsa, Camp de Mar* and *Andraitx* harbour.

The buses that go to *Coll d'en Rabassa* and *Ca'n Pastilla* start just outside the railway station of *Sóller.* And those going to *Coll d'en Rabassa. Playa de Palma* and *El Arenal* leave from *Reina Constanza* street (off *Primo de Rivera* avenue).

EXCURSION TO GENOVA AND NA BURGUESA. — *Génova* is a picturesque hamlet which has become a favorite with the tourists situated at 6 kms. from *Palma* with its primitive cottages scatered all over the mountain side. Starting at this little place a road leads to the oratory of *Na Burguesa* 300 m. high on the mountain, where you get a beautiful view of the town with the vast plain and huge bay, having the *Bellver* castle in the foreground.

VIEWS OF BELLVER CASTLE.

Entrance to the Castle

West façade.

BELLVER CASTLE. — Of all the excursions around the town this one is the most interesting and the easiest to carry out. Over 200.000 people visit the castle every year. One can go half way by bus, which leaves from *Plaza de la Reyna*, getting off at *Son Armadams*. From there a nice road, about one km. long, will take you through the woods up to the castle located on a small hill 140 meters high. There is plenty of parking space. There is also another road that starts at *Plaza de Gomila*, that goes to the castle.

It dates back to the 14th century and was erected by James II, King of Majorca, under the superintendence of *Pedro Salvá.* It served as a summer residence for the Kings of Majorca and after their defeat at the battle of *Lluchmayor* in 1349 it served as a prison for the family of James III, who perished in the battle. John I of Aragon settled there with his family in 1395 when he fled from an epidemic raging in Catalonia. The castle was besieged and stormed by the "Agermanats" and then served as a prison, first for state prisoners and afterwards for common criminals. At the beginning of the 18th cen-

Entrance from Homenage Tower.

Castle courtyard.

tury a number of French prisoners captured in the War of Independence were kept there. From 1801 until 1807 the well-known Jovellanos was there as a prisoner and there, too, he wrote his best works. A memorial stone in the room he ocupied and a bust out in the wood are tokens of the presence of the illustrious writer. On July 5, 1817, following orders, *General Lacy*, a man of liberal ideas, was shot there. In the same castle died, in 1824, the great patriots Boned and Coll. In 1852 it was visited by the Duke of Montpensier and in 1860 by Queen Elisabeth II of Spain and in 1903 by King Alfonso XIII.

According to Jovellanos it is one of the best military monuments of the 15th century and is well preserved. In shape it is circular and posesses four towers, apart from four more of larger size and outside the main castle itself. It is surrounded with a double moat. The outer line of defense is modern (17th century).

The castle has a large central courtyard, also circular, where the well stands, and a very wide corridor linking all the rooms. In the lower part the arches are semicircular and in the upper, pointed. (Gothic). The castle is entirely covered by a terrace roof. Inside, somewhat restored, is found the Chapel with its wooden barrier dating back to the building of the castle.

Standing apart from the main body of the Castle is the *Torre del Homenaje* (Tower of Homage) which is connected by two arched bridges with the Castle itself. In this tower are located one above the other, a series of gloomy dungeons — especially depressing is the lowest one whose only communication with the outside world is a hole above, which serves at the same time as door and window, hence its name "La Olla" (the pot).

From the terrace and even more from the lofty towers we enjoy a view over a wide landscape, dominating on one side the wide bay, the Island of *Cabrera* and the port, as well as below, at the foot of the Castle, the wood, *Terreno* and *Porto Pi* with their houses; on the other side are the plain and the mountain range with its lofty peaks. The City now-a-days owns the Castle and the wood an *Bellver's* beautiful rooms serve as a worthy frame for the museum they house. In the museum there are relics from excavations as well as what remains of the Museum, once existing at *Raxa*.

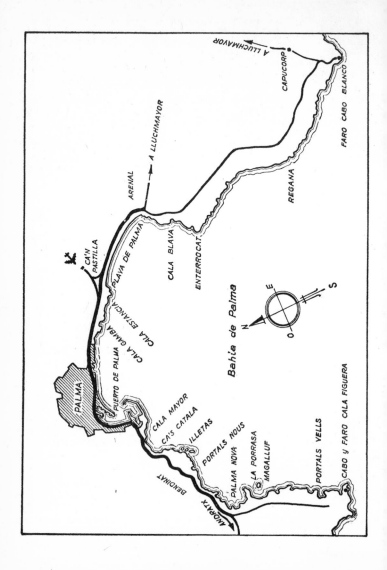

Cala Mayor.

EXCURSION THROUGH THE MARITIME ZONE
OF PALMA

The bay of *Palma*, from *Cabo Blanco* to *Cala Figuera*, are the extremes that with their respective lighthouses determine the entrance to the bay, with a seaboard of about 60 kms. *Palma* as a city has a maritime forefront of some 20 kms. forming a terrace over the ocean, that extends from *Ca's Catalá* to *El Arenal*. Both extremes are binded by a marvelous avenue, essentially maritime, including a number of sections that were built over land gained to the ocean.

Taking as point of departure the entrance to the city from the buildings where maritime services are installed and a monument to Ramón Llull erected, we can make two magnificent tours without loosing sight of the ocean, one to the East and another to the West, two excursions very interesting to do in a morning or afternoon. During the summer months there is great competition between the two touristic zones that do their best to attract more tourists to their respective beaches.

Beach of *Illetas*.

Beach of *Portals Nous*.

Palma Nova.

Going through the West Coast. — Beginning at the already mentioned site we find the *Sagrera* promenade with her tall palm trees and monumental buildings of *La Lonja* and *Consulado del Mar*, already described. Then we reach a big square with beautiful gardens and close to it is the *Club Náutico*, which manifests the Majorcan fondness for the nautical sport, modern buildings with magnificent rooms, terraces and the piers where thousands of boats are berthed, between which we count hundreds of yachts, most of them foreign.

Afterwards we enter the maritime promenade, 3 kms. long, that connects the commercial port with the big wharf for transatlantic liners. Opposite to the shore is a thick line of new and high buildings, most of them first class hotels. To the end of the promenade and in contrast with the modern constructions we find the *Torre de Pelaires*, a historical monument of XV century that for so many centuries constituted the defense of *Porto Pi*, the primitive port of *Palma*, and today, distant from the ocean by the construction of new piers with maritime stations.

Past the tower, continuing on the same avenue we will come to an intersection where we will take the road that leads to the West jetty. Here is a commercial port, 2 kms, long, for draught vessels. The avenue continues through the former *Andraitx* road. All over we will see a saturation of hotels, apart-

Magalluf.

Santa Ponsa.

Majorcan country people. -

Harbour of *Soller*. -

Santa Ponsa.

ment buildings, stores, coffee shops, bars, travel agencies, etc., with an immense traffic. In km. 5 and dominating the ocean we find *Marivent*, summer residence of H. M. the King of Spain. Between km. 6 & 7 there is the tiny beach of *Cala Mayor* the district of *San Agustín* and *Ca's Catalá*, where the urban zone of *Palma* ends.

It is worth to continue the excursion through the same road that goes through *Portals* (km. 9), until km. 14, entering then in *Palma Nova*, a residential, touristic and hotel area with excellent beaches and complex boulevards between shady pine trees. Following the main avenue and without loosing sight of the ocean that extends for about 1 km., we will arrive in *Magalluf*, another big urbanization. These two urbanizations are connected to each other by excellent boulevards skirted by the fine white beaches. Continuing on the same avenue and without loosing sight of the ocean we come to *Portals Vells* and almost to the lighthouse of *Cala Figuera*, where we must then consider this as the end of the trip through the Western part of the bay of *Palma*. The liveliness in these beaches during the summer months is superb. Sometimes it is difficult to find accommodations in the buses and even a place to bathe on the beach.

← *Cala Pi.*

← *Castle of Bellver.*

Ca'n Pastilla.

Ca'n Pastilla.

El Arenal promenade.

Going through the East Coast. — Starting at the *Sagrera* promenade to the opposite direction and following the big avenue that borders the ocean we see the beginning of the highway that leads to the airport. Going through we can see and admire the monuments over the walls that form the gothic palace of *La Almudaina,* the cathedral, the Episcopal palace, and the manorial palaces of *La Portella.* Then after two more kilometers we are in *Portitxol,* the fishermen's port. Here we can continue on the same Road or go through to *Molinar & Coll d'en Rabassa,* both roads leading to *Ca'n Pastilla* (km. 7). This is a touristic spot that for its liveliness during the summer is similar to the centre of a big city. Now begins a 5 km. avenue with the beach on one side *(Playa de Palma)* and opposite to it a compact tier of hotels, bars, stores for all tastes, and ending at *El Arenal,* 12 kms. from *Palma.* The proximity to the city and the good public service contribute a great deal to the liveliness of this 5 kms. of beaches and avenue during the summer.

About half way between *Ca'n Pastilla* and *El Arenal* at a short distance from the sea shore, we find the church *La Porciuncula,* of the Franciscan Order to which belonged the great philosopher Ramón Llull and the evangelizer of California, Fray Junípero Serra. This church is situated on high land in a beautiful park of pine trees, it is of modern construction, based

Ca'n Pastilla.

El Arenal.

El Arenal Yacht Club.

on the Gothic style. Its walls are all of stained glass windows, it is the most original conception of our local architect Ferragut.

If we wish to complete the excursion, we can continue on the same road, skirting the ocean and passing through *Cala Blava, Enterrocat & Regana* and ending at the lighthouse of *Cabo Blanco* (32 kms.) This part does not have the interest of atmosphere of the first 12 km. Three kilometres north of *Cabo Blanco*, going through the *Lluchmayor* road, we find the pre-historic town of *Capucorp*, which is worth visiting if interested in primitive constructions.

If we want to go as far a *Cala Pi*, about 7 kms. from the bay of *Palma*, and through a magnificent road after *Cabo Blanco*, we must follow the road to *Lluchmayor* until we come to an intersection leading to *Vallgomera* and staying always in the right we will come to *Cala Pi*. Here you will see a beautiful, beach where you will enjoy the smooth waters of this enchanted and colourful corner of our island.

Majorcan typical kitchen.

Sini (Majorcan noria).

CHAPTER III

INLAND EXCURSIONS

A visit to Majorca, however short as it may be, should not and cannot be confined to the town, the most interesting features of the visit are the island excursions. Not to take any excursions amounts to not visiting Majorca at all. A 2.000 kms. road network enables the visitor to drive around. To make one's own car available will always be the best plan. Several thousands of privately owned cars are thus taken onto the island yearly. Besides there exist firms in *Palma* dealing with motorcycle or self-drive cars.

A complete touring organisation has been established selling individual tickets for all the excursions. The coaches leave the town between 9 and 10 a.m. driving round to the main hotels to collect the passengers. In the evening they take them back to their hotels. The most popular excursions being; the trip to *Valldemosa,* with a visit to the Carthusian Monastery; the trip to *Manacor,* visiting the grottoes of Drach and Hams; the one to *Pollensa* and *Formentor;* the visit to the grottoes of *Artá;* and the trip to *Lluch* and *Torrent de Pareis.* All these excursions, and many others are made in comfortable coaches with guide-interpreter. Tickets are sold in travel agencies and in most of the hotels.

A convenient system in the absence of one's own car is for five or six persons to hire a car from any of the Renta-a-Car Agencies through-out the island. This system proves to be the most convenient, economical and enjoyable being that you plan your own excursions and you are at leisure to enjoy what interest you most. Take advantage being on your own to visit some of the Majorcan typical country houses close to the road, some of them wonderful mansions of XVII or XVIII century. In Spring and Summer the excursions as described in this guide book can be carried out in an afternoon. If the number of excursionists is big enough to fill up a car, this system besides being the most suitable turns out to be the cheapest.

8 kms. from where we started and on the right side, we pass *Bendinat,* a estate with beautiful gardens, where a palace was built in the XIX century. The road borders the seashore and along in we find several building sites, with modern buildings, hotels and restaurants. From *Palma* and as far a 25 kms. can be considerer as a residential touristic area, with its several beaches girdled with trees, facing south, warm during the winter and quite fresh during the summer.

The routes for the excursions described in this Guide follow the best main roads and visit the most interesting places from the tourist's point of view. However, today the cross-roads and divertions on all main roads have posted signs in such a way that nobody should get lost. So the excursions, with the variation which best suit the visitor, can be made with the general and complete map which we publish.

In the Summer, weather permitting, sea-excursions are carried out in comfortable boats leaving from the quay in front of *La Lonja* and sailing to the western coast enabling tripmakers to spend a few hours bathing at *Palma Nova* and *Magalluf* and other beaches.

Mountaineering amateurs can make splendid mountain excursions. These will be described in their corresponding chapter at the end.

No detailed prices or time tables of the different services can be given here as they are fixed beforehand at the beginning of each season.

PLACES INLAND OF TOURIST INTEREST AND THEIR DISTANCE FROM PALMA

Alfabia gardens	17	kms.
Artá Caves	81	»
Campanet Caves	37	»
Drach Caves	63	»
Hams Caves	61	»
Génova Caves	6	»
Deyá	27	»
Galilea	21	»
Lluch monastery	47	»
Miramar	22	»
Orient	26	»
Randa sanctuary	36	»
Raxa gardens	13	»
Son Marroig	24	»
San Salvador sanctuary	27	»
Son Sanjuán airport	9	»
Valldemosa	17	»
Valldemosa hermitage	21	»

MAIN BEACHES, RESIDENTIAL SEASIDE RESORTS, AND THEIR DISTANCES FROM PALMA

Ca'n Pastilla	7	kms.
Arenal	13	»
Cala Blava	20	»
Colonia de San Jorge	52	»
Cala Santanyi	55	»
Cala Figuera	55	»
Porto Petro	58	»
Cala d'Or	70	»
Porto Colom	62	»
Porto Cristo	62	»
L'Illot	67	»
Cala Millor	70	»
Canyamel	80	»
Cala Ratjada	80	»
Ca'n Picafort	64	»
Puerto de Alcudia	55	»
Puerto de Pollensa	60	»
Formentor	70	»
Cala San Vicente	60	»
La Calobra and Torrent de Pareis	71	»
Puerto de Sóller	35	»
San Telmo	37	»
Puerto de Andraitx	35	»
Camp de Mar	27	»
Paguera	23	»
Santa Ponsa	19	»
Magalluf	16	»
Palma Nova	14	»
Portals Nous	10	»
Illetas	3	»

For the full map of the island see Mapa general de Mallorca, by J. MASCARO PASARIUS.

MALLORCA

D. Corbella

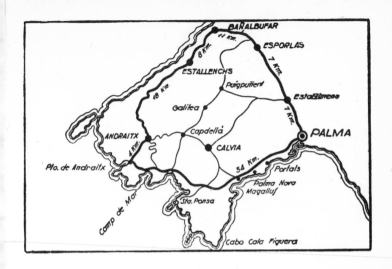

FIRST EXCURSION: PALMA - CAMP DE MAR - ANDRAITX & ITS PORT - ESTALLENCHS - BAÑALBUFAR - ESPORLAS - ESTABLIMENS - PALMA (89 kms. long round trip)

We start out along the road skirting the western part of the bay past *Terreno*, *Porto Pi* and *Cala Mayor;* places already mentioned in the previous excursion. As far as *Hotel Maricel*, 7 kms. from *Palma* can be considered as a street of the city with buildings on both sides and ending the township.

8 kms. from where we started and on the right side, we pass *Bendinat*, a estate with beautiful gardens, where a palace was built in the XIX century. The road borders the seashore and along in we find several building sites, with modern buildings, hotels and restaurants. From *Palma* and as far as 25 kms. can be considered as a residential touristic area, with its several beaches girdled with trees, facing south, warm during the winter and quite fresh during the summer.

Santa Ponsa. Houses.

Santa Ponsa. Cross commemorating the landing of King James I.

Paguera.

and *Santa Ponsa* 17 kms. which conserves remains of gothic fortifications and a beautiful garden of palm-trees. 23 kms. from
Palma we find *Paguera* a beautiful summer resort, full of villas
and residential houses on the border of the sea, 25 kms. from
Palma we find *Camp de Mar* with its beach of fine sand.

On this road there is a zone full of historic remains. On the
10th of September 1229 the King Don Jaime I known as "El Conquistador" landed with all his army at "La Caleta" off *Santa
Ponsa*. The spot is now marked by a large cross. From this point
the army began the conquest of the island. Several battles
were fought, the most important being the victory of the "Coll
de la Batalla" at 16 kms., where the two brothers Moncada lost
their lives; the consequence of this battle was that *Palma* was
beseiged and conquered on the 31 December of the same year
by the Christian army. Near this place and inside a little oratory
recently built, we can find the "Piedra Sagrada" that was used
as an altar by the bishop of *Barcelona*, Berenguer de Palou,
when the first mass after the battle was said.

30 kms. from *Palma* we reach *Andraitx*, village of 6.000 inhabitants placed at the bottom of a valley and centre of numerous
excursions. The most important of them are: The harbour
itself (5 kms. by road). *S'Arracó* and *San Telmo* (7 kms. by road)
and Trapa 2 hours on foot from *S'Arracó*. A maritime excursion
can be organized either from *Andraitx* harbour or *San Telmo*,

Camp de Mar.

Andraitx harbour.

La Dragonera isle.

both fishing hamlets, to the *Dragonera*, an islet 7 kms. long and with a hill of 300 m. with a lighthouse, separated from Majorca by a two miles sea channel.

To complete the trip we recommend readers to leave *Camp de Mar* and proceed directly to the harbour by road at the kms. 25 out of *Palma* and keep left as far as *Andraitx* (5 kms.); then we continue the trip to *Andraitx*. In all these places hotels and restaurants can be found.

The distance between *Andraitx* and *Estallenchs* is 18 kms. The road recently built passes through *Coma Freda* and the *Coll de Sa Gramola*, from where a beautiful landscape can be seen. Leaving behind the cliffs *Cap Fabiolé* the road is of modern lay-out and lies always at great height through pine woods, on arriving at the tunnel *El Grau* where we have the most beautiful view of the Mediterranean from the *Mirador Ricardo Roca*, situated over the mountain.

Estallenchs is a small village with typical streets and several excursions can be carried out from this point.

On along the same road, along the cliffs of the north coast, we come to *La Atalaia de las Ánimas*, one of the old watch towers built during the XVI century along the coast to prevent the raids of pirates. From these towers one can enjoy a grand view over the mountain range from *La Dragonera* as far as *Sóller*.

Flank of Estallenchs.

Mirador Ricardo Roca (between *Andraitx-Estallenchs*).

Bañalbufar.

Bañalbúfar, placed at 8 kms. from *Estallenchs* is worthy of mention because of its situation on the side of the mountain, and is a magnificent example of the works of man who has built on the hillside countless terraces. It is a notable tomato growing centre and which forms its chief source of wealth. From this village an excursion can be made to the seashore at Port *d'Es Canonge* not far away.

Passing through thick and shady woods, but always overlooking the sea, the road makes its way alongside the mountains until suddenly the scenery changes and among the thick groves of olive trees, which we enter shortly before arriving at *Esporlas*, we find the *Granja* estate, a magnificent country house standing in its own extensive grounds which are ornamented by many fountains. The road now passes through *Esporlas* —14 kms. from *Palma*— where at 3 kms. on the outskirts we find the *Canet* estate. This estate is remakable on account of its fine gardens and large pond. The road continues by *Coll d'En Portell*, from there we behold the city, and on through tilled fields leaving on the right the estate of *Sarriá* and *Buñolí* — another estate with stately country mansion. After having driven through *Establimens* we find ourselves again in *Palma*.

Esporlas. Gallery of *La Granja.*

SECOND EXCURSION: PALMA - VALLDEMOSA - MIRAMAR - DEYA - SOLLER & ITS PORT - COLL DE SOLLER - ALFABIA - RAXA - PALMA (78 kms. long round trip)

This excursion is also a round trip and can be made either by car or by bus normally operating this service.

Starting from *Palma* the road lies through cultivated fields where many almond trees are encountered. One km. out we reach *s'Esglaieta,* a mere handful of houses beyond which thousand year old olive trees begin to be met. 13 kms. from *Palma* the scenery changes abrupfly. Two lofty cliffs —*S'Estret* (the Narrow Pass)— mark the beginning of the mountainous area. The road keeps rising and leaves below on the left the *Son Brondo* valley with its abundant greenery. 17 kilometers from *Palma* is *Valldemosa,* a pleasant village 400 meters high. On acount of its situation it is cool in summer and close to the capital — it has always been the favorite resort of the well-to-do.

Harbour of *Soller.* →

Typical majorcan house →

Valldemosa

La Real Cartuja (Royal Carthusian Convent), was founded in 1339 by King Martin who relinquished the palace of the Kings of Mallorca for the purpose of founding the convent. Of the Palace and the old monastery nothing remains now. The cloister —Cloister of St. Mary— which is the oldest part and the buildings around in date from the XVIII century and should be visited. The neo-classical church is ornamented with fresco paintings by Fray Bayeux; it has some remarkable choir stalls and the Pietá of the High Altar is the work of the sculptor Adrián Ferrá. In the sacristy a reliquary of rich ornaments embroidered with gold and silver and an altar screen made of plaster are to be noted. In the cloister the old pharmacy with its 17th century phials and jars preserving some of the drugs dating from the time of the Carthusian monks who lived there until the year 1853, is kept intact. Here, lived during the winter of 1838-39 the celebrated novelist Georges Sand in company of her son and daughter, and the famous musician Chopin who composed here some of his well-known Preludes.

At *Valldemosa* St. Catherine Thomas was born and her birthplace is still preserved together with plenty of souvenirs of this 16th century majorcan Saint.

At *Valldemosa* one can find a number of estates with their stately country dwellings. The chief ones are: *Pastoritx, Son Pax, Son Brondo, Son Salvat, Son Maixella, Son Puig, Sa Coma, Son Gual, Son Moragues, Son Ferrandell, Son Mas del Pla del Rei,* etc., besides the Archduke's at *Miramar.*

Mill of *Santa María.*

Camp de Mar.

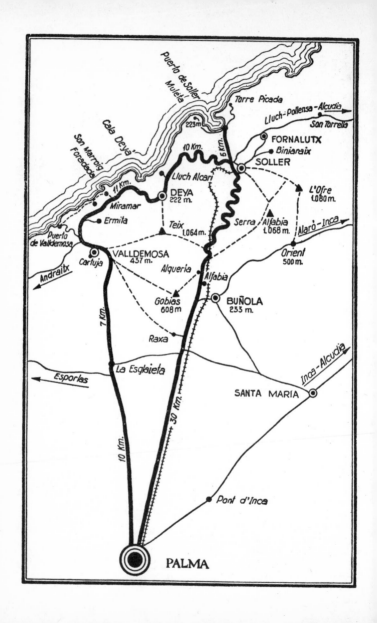

Valldemosa. La Cartuja.

Valldemosa is the starting point for many mountain excursions. A list of them would be practically endless. One such excursion towards the sea and the so called Port of *Valldemosa* can be carried out.

Leaving *Valldemosa* and along the same road, on the mountain side and skirting the sea, we motor on towards *Deyá* and 3 kms. away we find *Miramar*. This is the name by which the large area, consisting of a dozen estates, which was bougth by Archduke Louis Salvador of Austria at the end of the last century, is known. It formed a single estate with great woods laced with paths leading here and there to the splendid belvederes which the Prince had built on the imposing rocks to view the sea in all its splendor. He rendered these rocks easily accessible and thanks to his artistic gifts, embellished the landscape. We recommend to the tourist to look out from at least one of these vantage points — veritable balconies hanging over the sea — for example, that of *Sas Pitas,* close to the road at kilometer post 21. From here he will get some idea of the Archduke's happy conception. There are several dozen such observatories and to enumerate them would take too long. From the 20 kms. post starts a path leading to *La Ermita* (The Hermitage), half an hour away from the road with a remarkable panorama of the sea and the woods nearby. One is kindly welcomed by the hermits. Walking down towards the sea we can carry on the excursion to the Port of *Valldemosa* and to

La Cartuja. Cell-Museum of Chopin & George Sand.

La Cartuja. Cell-Museum of Chopin & George Sand.

La Cartuja. Farmacy of the Carthusian monks.

S'Estaca and *Font Figuera* too, the trail leading there starts at kilometer post 25 and to *Na Foradada* as well. On the *Miramar* estate some works from the Archduke's collection of art treasures as well as a Gothic altar screen are to be found. It was there, at *Miramar*, that Raymond Llull founded in the 13th century his centre of study, the famous "Escola de Llengües Orientals" (Oriental Languages School).

Further along the road still overlooking the sea, we reach *Son Marroig* a beautiful estate 24 kms. from *Palma*, where numerous relics of the Archduke are preserved, a little marble temple and belvedere with a magnificent view on to *Na Foradada*. 25 kms. from *Palma* we come to *Sa Pedrissa* and 4 kms. further on to *Deyá*, a charming hamlet with its typical houses spread out over the hillside. Due to its very particular situation *Deyá* is the starting point for a number of excursions through the mountains. The most interesting one is to the *Teix* at a height of over 1.000 m. Towards the sea the most noteworthy ones are to *Son Bujosa* and the *Deyá* Cove. Continuing along our road, one kilometer further on we come to *Lluch-Alcari*, a group of typical houses, surrounded with gardens and a resort of well-known painters.

The road continues along the flanks of the mountain and 38 kms. from *Palma* we arrive at the well-known *Valle de los Naranjos* (Valley of the Orange Trees), where we will find the

Valldemosa. Folkloric group *El Parado.*

town of *Sóller* (10.500 inh.) and where you could also find a lot of wealthy merchants who are owners of fruit shops in France and Belgium, and import this commodity. This commercial trade is among the main sources of wealth that have brought the town to be one of the richest and more modernized of the island.

SOLLER. — Is a centre for very interesting rambles. Just 1 km. away is *Son Angelats,* with notable gardens and country mansions; then we come to *Pujol d'en Banya* and *Tres Creus,* two heights dominating the town; and to *Sa Font de S'Olla.* A thick valley stretches out towards the peak of *Puig Mayor,* where we find *Fornalutx* (5 kms.), a typical village with steep paved strangely laid out streets and very close to it is *Binibassi* and *Biniaraitx,* two hamlets of singular character where starts a path leading to *El Barranc* (The gorge) and to the houses of *L'Ofre* (800 m.) and from where we can start to ascend to *Puig de l'Ofre* (1.090 m.).

Among the number of mountain excursions possible to carry out from *Sóller* we will mention the most interesting ones: Along the coast we can start an interesting ramble to *Balitx* and from where we can take a path that leads to *La Calobra* and *Torrent de Pareis.* It takes six hours to walk along the path stretching out along the picturesque scenery of the coast. It is much to be regretted that we still lack a road which would

Deyá. Son Marroig.

connect *Sóller* or the port with the present road leading to *Lluch* from *La Calobra* (28 kms.).

The most interesting mountain excursion that can be made from *Sóller* is the "Cornador". A cart track starts from in front of the cementery and leads to *Ses Piquetes de S'Arrom*, houses built at the height of some 600 meters where one finds the mirador *Joaquín Quesada* which dominates the immense valley formed by *Sóller, Fornalutx* and *Biniaraitx*. From the other side one can contemplate the higher points of the chain that forms a sort of amphitheatre *(Teix, Serra de Alfabia, L'Ofre* and *Puig Mayor)*. One can descend in the other direction since the same path continues until the houses of *L'Ofre* and here to the *Barranc* and so to *Biniaraitx* and from here to *Sóller*. The path is very easy and forms a circuit of about 20 kms. which can be covered in some 6 or 7 hours on foot.

Let us now leave *Sóller* and continue our excursion by the same road that brought us there, 5 kms. from the town we come to the Port. It is a fishermen's village, and a summer resort — a favorite place for long stays with its fine beach.

From the port of *Sóller* several excursions can be undertaken. The notable are those to the *Torre Picada*, and old watch tower well situated 2 kms. away, and to *Muleta*, opposite the harbour where the lighthouse stands.

An interesting set excursion to *La Calobra* and *Torrente de Pareis* can be undertaken. It takes only one hour to get there,

Deyá.

Harbour of *Soller:*

Harbour of *Soller*.

but as the *Calobra* cove is not properly sheltered a calm sea and fine weather are required so as to make sure it will be possible to land and eventually to re-embark at *La Calobra*.

The return from the Port of *Sóller* is by the same road. We soon pass through *Sóller* and immediately beyond starts the swift ascent, the road zigzags rapidly up to the *Sóller* Pass — 400 m. high. Nearby stands a very remarkable Gothic cross. Once over the pass we lose sight of the Valley of *Sóller* and the *Puig Mayor* and new scenery comes into view. On the south side of the mountain, far away in the distance dominating the plain, we can see *Palma*. The road then winds down in great curves to the foot of the mountain and there, on the plain, stands *Alfabia* — a great house, more accurately a palace, it is well worth visiting with is magnificent gardens and fountains. The house stands among shady trees. The ceiling of the hall is of Moorish style. It is panelled and bears inscriptions.

The 17 kms. road from *Alfabia* to *Palma* lies across the plain among the olive trees. On our left we leave the village of *Buñola* with streets and houses typical of the region and on the right *Biniforani*, *S'Alquería*, *Son Narci* and *Binietzar*. 12 kms. from *Palma* we come to *Raxa* notable on account of its mansion and gardens. These were the work of Cardinal *Despuig* at the close of the 18th century. The pond and the monumental

Clastre (courtyard) in *Raxa*.

Italian style staircase should be seen. After crossing *Son Sardina* we find ourselves once more in *Palma* at the end of our 78 kms. circuit.

This excursion is amongst the most essential ones that take place from the town to the various places of the island. There is no doubt that the generosity of Archduke Luis Salvador of Austria has contributed to the present charm of this place. It was in 1880 that this man made one of his houses into a hostel, situated by the road at 21 km. from *Palma*. This hostel was named *Ca Madó Pilla* after the peasant woman who ran it. It no longer exists, in its place there is a modern hotel. In this hostel, anyone could have a bed, avail himself of the kitchen facilities, and have oil, olives, at will, all free of charge for three days; what he founded was similar to the "parador de turismo" of to day (Tourist hostel), of which there are so many in the mainland (all hotels of Majorca are privately run). His main concern was that everybody could avail himself of the facilities of his properties, and could stroll through his lands of *Miramar*. In contrast with this generous attitude we have a number of the present owners, nouveaux riches, who put up signs of "No trespassers" by the road side. A concept of the Middle Ages over the property applied in modern times.

Raxa. Lake in the gardens.

Alfabia.

139

Selva. Parish Church

Pollensa. Cala San Vicente

Lluch Monastery.

Pollensa. Way up to *El Calvario.*

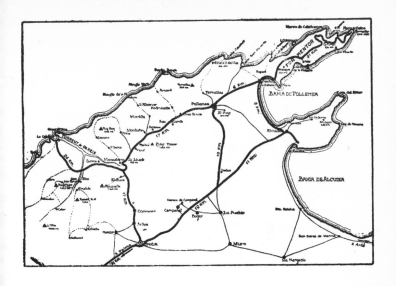

THIRD EXCURSION: PALMA - INCA - MONASTERY OF LLUCH - POLLENSA - CALA SAN VICENTE - PUERTO DE POLLENSA - FORMENTOR LIGHTHOUSE - ALCUDIA - PORT OF ALCUDIA (Whole circuit: 185 kms. long)

On leaving *Palma* the old road runs north-easterly, 5 kms. from *Palma* we pass through the first village, *Pont d'Inca*, and then we leave *Son Bonet*, airport, on our right. Between 9 and 10 kms. from *Palma* to the right of the road and 200 meters from it stands *Son Verí*, which may be visited with a noteworthy collection of paintings and objects of art.

15 kms. from *Palma* we come to *Santa María* where we visit the church, noteworthy for her "baroque" doors and the Town-Hall of the same style. By law of nature the first road that must have existed in the island was that which linked the primitive towns of the Roman foundations Palmaria (known now as *Palma*) and Pollentia (now *Alcudia*). This village was a halt on the road which joined the above villages and for this reason took the name *Santa María del Camí* (road) which still exists.

Lluch-Pollensa road.

From here a very interesting excursion can be undertaken to *Coa Negre.* There is *Son Torrella* — a country house in purest Majorcan style. After two hours walking *Avenc de Son Pou* is reached. In this estate is a tremendous grotto and the sunrays entering through a hole in the roof, produces an effect of pure fantasy. The excursion can be prolonged along the *Freu* to *Orient* and from there we can reach *Buñola* by road (10 kms.). Here is a station of the *Sóller* railway. Alternatively, starting from *Son Pou* we can retrace our footsteps to *Santa María.*

From *Santa María* the road runs parallel to the railway through Consell, noteworthy for hand-made esparto sandals, and *Binisalem,* well known on account if its famous wines. At *Lloseta,* which we leave on the left, is the mansion and orchard of *Ayamans,* now-a-days owned by the *March* family who has restored the palace in splendid style. They are worth a visit.

INCA (18.000 inhabitants) is 20 kms. from *Palma.* It is situated in the centre of the island and it is the chief town of the district, very important as an' agricultural centre. Every Thursday a busy market is held there, and the November fair is very well-known, especially the *Dijous Bò,* the most important among all the agricultural shows held in Majorca. But up-to-date in this modern world, this famous fair has been

Pollensa. Roman bridge.

overshadowed by an exhibition of modern machinery and the buying and selling of second-hand cars. There are textile mills and an important shoe and leather industry. A large number of workers with self transportation come to *Inca* every day from the neighbouring villages to work in the important workshops.

Notable is the Parish church of *Santa María la Mayor,* with its gothic style bell-tower and altar decorations, constructed like the cloisters of the monasteries of *San Francisco* and *Santo Domingo* in the XVIII century. The most important thing remaining from the old village is the inn *Son Fuster* and the nuns convent of *San Jerónimo,* where they sell the famous *"concos d'Inca",* the only *cake of its kind.* The typical entrance with its bell-tower remains. There are the classic "cellers'", the ancient wine vaults, with their traditional barrels. Here are served roast sucking pig (porsella rostida), and the local dish of fried lamb, they are moreover tourist haunts which, in their local atmosphere, serve the same dishes as any of the other island restaurants.

The centre of the town has undergone a series of reforms, consisting of the demolition of houses in order to widen the streets; with this modernization it has lost most of its character. *Inca* is today a modern and prosperous industrial town, with a magnificent market, cinemas, cafes, bars and important

Harbour of *Pollensa*.

businesses of every description. The only excursion is to the hermitage of *Santa Magdalena*, some 5 kms. from the town.

Fron *Inca* we continue our route to *Selva* and to *Caimari* where the scenery changes. Mountainous now, the road winds up among woods and rocks to a height of 500 m. 17 kms. from *Inca* stands the Monastery of *Lluch*, built in a fertile valley at a height of 400 m. and surrounded with high mountains and thick woods.

In the monastery the little statue of the Virgin Mary known as *La Moreneta* is kept. It enjoys a great devotion among the Majorcan people and has always been object of traditional pilgrimages. The Monastery has recently been restored and so its ancient character has been lost. It contains a large hostelery. Its cloister or main square is specially worth noting.

Lluch is a starting point for several excursions to *Sóller* (already described) and to *Torrent de Pareis* which will be described later. Apart from these, the most interesting is that passing through *Clot d'Albarca* and leading to *Casconá*, there is a house built under a rock. From here we can return via *Mossa*, following the track which winds around *Puig Roig* and overlooks the sea. This excursion, on foot, takes six hours. Another aim for a walk from *Lluch* is a visit to the Mystery Monuments situated on a neighbouring hill, and to *Font Cuberta*.

The trip to *Lluch* from *Palma* is well worth a whole day — specially when we use the combined service *Palma-Inca* by

Gardens at *Alfabia*. →

Raxa Clastre →

Pollensa. Bay of *Formentor.*

train and *Inca-Lluch* by bus. Thanks to its elevated situation and its coolness, many families spend the summer at *Lluch* and make it a lively place.

Leaving *Lluch* we can continue our journey to *Pollensa* by a fine recently built road which starts at 400 m., rising to a height of 700 m. at *Femeninas* and then runs through the mountainous region between *Puig Roig* and *Puig Tomer* — both over 1.000 m. high. The road then winds down the fertile valley *d'En March,* where the landscape with its abundant vegetation contrasts sharply with the mountainous region just crossed, 18 kms. from *Lluch* we come to *Pollensa* — a place much favored by painters.

POLLENSA. — Has plenty of noteworthy features and picturesque surroundings which can be the aims of many excursions. The principal ones are:

To *Calvario* (Calvary) on the hill flanking *Pollensa.* The road to the top of the hill is most picturesque with its double row of cypress trees. From the little oratory, above, a wide view is obtained.

The *Oratory* of *El Puig* 300 m. high is 3 kms. further on and an inn and a hermitage are to be found there. Visitors are kindly welcomed. Access is easy and the ascent last one hour. From there we dominate the bays of *Pollensa* and *Alcudia* and, in clear weather, can see the island of Menorca.

← *Raxa.* Stairs to the Gardens.

← *Pollensa.* Way up to *El Calvario.*

Pollensa. Beach of *Formentor.*

The *Castell del Rei* (King's Castle), which we reach via the *Tarnellas* valley and a mule-track about 6 kms. long, possesses *La Cella*, an old hermitage, and the remains of an ancient Moorish castle. This fortress, often besieged in the past, has a magnificent situation on a great rocky promontory 400 m. high falling abruptly to the sea. It is a good place from which to view the lofty cliffs of the northern coast.

The valley *d'En March* on the road leading to *Lluch* is itself the starting point for other excursions — for example that from *Som Grua* which passes through *Pedruixella* and leads to the *Torre d'Ariant* and its wild rock the *Single Verd* which is situated at a great height on the cliffs in a little frequented spot. The excursion to *Mortix* and *L'Albanor* and on to *El Single del Pi* lasts two hours; its sets off along the same road and is as charming as the preceding ones.

Continuing along the *Pollensa* road to the port we find 2 kms. away on the left the road leading to *Cala San Vicente*. This picturesque spot is 4 kms. away and possesses a lovely beach which stretches in Dantesque fashion below the cliffs of *Cavall Bernat;* it has been put on canvas by countless painters. Carrying on along the *Pollensa* road, 7 kms. from the town itself we come to the port, a populous village once exclusively inhabited by fishermen but now a summer tourist resort with 4 kms. of sea front lined with magnificent villas and hotels. From the port one can make the excursion to *Cala Vall de Boquer*, a one

Formentor Lighthouse.

hour's walk down a path winding through the mountains, and to *Cala San Vicente* by a short cut which takes an hour on foot.

As for sea trips the tourist can hire motor canoes and sail for *Sas Caletas* on the other side of the bay, on the flank of Mount Victoria and below the sanctuary of la Victoria; another trip can be carried out to *Formentor* and the lighthouse, admiring the greatness of that wild area with its nests of big birds.

FORMENTOR. — The road runs through the hamlet of *Puerto de Pollensa* and immediately after leaving the village it begins to rise. The panorama changes completely after port of *Pollensa*. We are now in the middle of *Costa Brava*. The pinewoods stretch away for several square kilometers, 10 kms. from *Puerto de Pollensa,* and in this wilderness is a beach of fine sands and the hotel *Formentor*.

FORMENTOR LIGHTHOUSE. — If Majorca were a continent we could say that *Formentor* is a peninsula terminating in cape *Formentor* the extreme north of the island. The road, of recent construction goes right to where the lighthouse stands, 13 kms. from the hotel, 23 kms. from *Puerto de Pollensa* and 83 from *Palma*. It is the farthest spot from the town. The 23 kms. road between *Puerto de Pollensa* and the lighthouse of *Formentor,* magnificently designed skirts the cliffs with their many belvede-

View from *Formentor* lighthouse.

res and commands a view of the sea on either side, from a height of 200 to 300 m. A tunnel of 200 m. goes through the mountain the *Es Fumat* 350 m. high. For wildness and grandeur, this route is without rival in Majorca. Shortly before reaching the tunnel and quite close to the road we find *Cala Murta*, a cove with transparent waters and fine sands. At this beautiful spot between the road and the shore the bust of the great Majorcan poet Costa y Llobera, the great bard of this part of the island is erected. The lighthouse, at an altitude of 209 m., forms a magnificent balcony overlooking the sea on three sides. From there one enjoys the largest view over the Mediterranean with all comfort. One looks out over the north coast from which just out The *Morro de Catalunya*. To the south are the two bays of *Pollensa* and *Alcudia* separated by the mountain *La Victoria* with the cape of *Ferrutx* in the distance. In clear weather one can see the island of *Menorca* with *Ciudadela* at the nearest point (40 kms.). Between Majorca and Menorca lies the immense sea which separates the two islands.

From *Formentor* lighthouse we must retrace our steps to *Pollensa* by our outward route and once more in this charming village we can continue our trip to *Alcudia;* all this region is rich in Roman remains and has been the object of numerous excavations. Some of the remains brought to light are in the Museum in *Palma*. Also found here were the remains of walls built in the Middle Ages. Two gateways have been preserved.

Alcudia. Doorway of *San Sebastián.*

From *Alcudia* we continue to the Port, 2 kms. away and situated on the inner bend of its fine bay. It has an admirable beach — the longest in the island. Departing from either *Alcudia* or the Port we can reach the *Victoria* shrine, 5 kms. from the village. It is situated on the mountain side with a beautiful view of the Bay of *Pollensa* and, in the background, *Formentor.*

At approximately 3 km. from the harbour and close to the road to *Artá,* we find the caves of *San Martín* a slope of about 20 meters. In these caves there are two small Gothic chapels one dedicated to Saint Martin, and the other to Saint George, being an original sanctuary very different to the others of the same style and period that exist on the island.

In the Port of *Alcudia* we are at our farthest from *Palma.* The road 55 kms. long forms a line dividing the island into two parts and it is by this same road that we return to *Palma.*

Alcudia. Wharf door.

Alcudia. The port.

Grottoes of Campanet. Interior.

GROTTOES OF CAMPANET. — Returning from *Alcudia* to *Palma* by the direct road, we can visit the grottoes of *Campanet*. To do this, we may choose between two roads; one branches off 30 kms. from *Palma* and the other 36'2 kms. By either road after 3 kms. we come to these magnificent grottoes, subterranean marvel well worth visiting. Discovered in 1948, they have been lit throughout by electricity. The underground path is 1.200 meters long. They can be visited with every comfort. Not very far from here is the oratory of *San Miguel*, one of Majorca's early christian churches. 25 kms. from the Port of *Alcudia* we reach *Inca* which we visited earlier and where we complete the circuit *Inca-Lluch-Pollensa-Alcudia-Inca* returning directly to *Palma* (20 kms.), by the same road on which we started out.

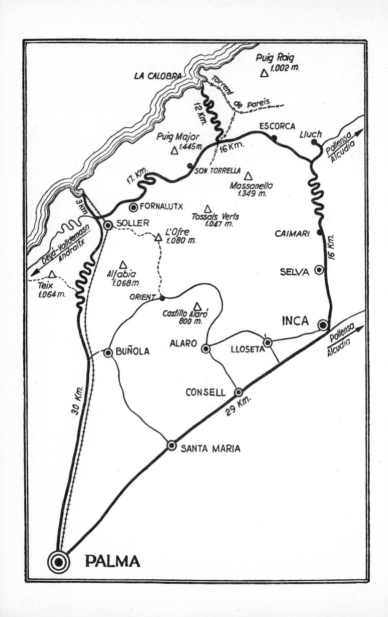

Soller-Lluch road.

FOURTH EXCURSION: PALMA - INCA - LLUCH - LA CALO-BRA AND TORRENT DE PAREIS - SON TORRELLA SOLLER - PALMA

The *Lluch Torrent*, gathering the water from the upper valleys of *Lluch*, and *Clot d'Aubarca*, and the *Gorg Blau* torrent which gathers the water from *Pla de Cuber* and the area between the mountains of *Puig Major* and *Massanella* unite in a single stream at *L'Entreforc* to make up the high *Torrent de Pareis* (Twin Torrent). At the foot of the high mountains an enormous split between them, is found the bed of this torrent. It is about 4 kms. long and the rocks rise from 300 to 400 m. wide. The shade cast by these enormous rocks upon the bed of the torrent is such that there is a spot, called *La Fosca* (Darkness).

It is much to be regretted that an excursion to such a picturesque spot has to be carried out under special weather condition. Broadly, it being impossible to walk upon the bed of the torrent during winter, the project must be undertaken during the summer when the bed is quite dry. Even so, it is difficult to cross and in any case it is impossible to climb up any of the steep rocks bordering it.

Torrent de Pareis.

To carry out the excursion and travel along the *Torrent* on foot we start from *Escorca* whose houses are near the *Lluch-La Calobra* road about 5 kms., from the Monastery. At this spot there is a splendid belvedere from which we can view the beach formed between the mountains by the waters, the mountains themselves forming the flanks of the torrent with the blue sea in the back-ground.

The footpath starts from *Escorca* and leads to *L'Entreforc* —already mentioned—in an hour. Here the true bed of the famous torrent—*Torrent de Pareis*—really begins. If the torrent is dry we can walk along its bed to the mouth. If it is not we must retrace our footsteps to *Escorca*. To reach the mouth of the torrent, if conditions are favorable, it takes four hours and even so, it is a difficult journey on account of the heat— summer being the only season in which it can be carried out. However, there is a very reason to claim that one has admired a natural wonder unique of its kind.

The excursion can be limited to a visit to the mouth of the *Torrent* starting from *La Calobra*. We can sail from the Port of *Sóller* in one of the boats running the regular service, the trip lasts an hour. But if we travel by this means we must first make sure that the sea is not rough in order that we may land. This trip is worth making for the view of high cliffs on the North coast.

Torrent de Pareis.

Nowadays the excursions by land can be done at any time of the year. You drive to *La Calobra* 70 kms. from *Palma*. A regular motor coach service runs the line on certain days enabling the tripmaker to make the excursions individually. From there, thanks to a 200 m. tunnel for pedestrians cut through the rocks, you can get to the bed of the torrent at its mouth where enormous rocks form a vast plan whose only exit is to the sea. We recommend a stop at *Escorca*. From this vantage point an impressive general view of the torrent and the whole area is obtained.

The return to *Palma* could be made by another road. On returning to *La Calobra*, once you are at the height of *Cala Els Reis* follow the two highest mountains of the island *Massanella* and *Puig Major*, and go as far as the mansions of *Torrella* (900 m. high). Continue along this road with the magnificent panoramic view over the valley of *Sóller*. One passes very near *Fornalutx*, until arriving at *Sóller*, and from there to *Palma* (see itinerary of the second excursion). The distance to go is approximately the same as the return journey from *Inca* and has the attraction of a round trip of some 155 kms.

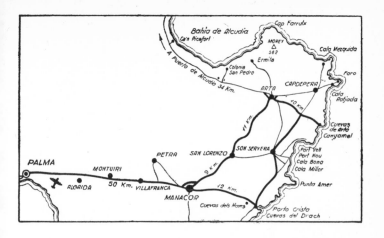

5th EXCURSION: HAMS, DRACH (MANACOR) AND ARTA GROTTOES

Touristically speaking, the easternmost area in the island is called grottoes area, for the most important grottoes in the island are situated there. Here we have a mountainous ground on which dry farming dominates. (Almond trees, and Carob bean trees.) Although a mountainous area it is independent from the main northern range. The mountains, many of them, crowned with thick pine groves are nowhere over 500 mts. high. In this region for so long subjected to pirate raids some of the estates still retain their all embattled defense towers. Such are *Canyamel* by the *Artá* grottoes, *Ses Puntas, Son Amoxa* and *Son Forteza* at *Manacor* and some others in the district of *Artá*.

The roads leading to the grottoes start from *Manacor*. A one day-visit to the grottoes allowing for the mileage will turn out to be somewhat hasty and tiring. A comfortable overnight stay at *Manacor, Porto Cristo* or *Canyamel* might be contemplated. On coach trips organized from *Palma* a visit to the *Hams* and *Drach* grottoes is scheduled on some days and on some other days another excursion to *Artá* grottoes. Besides these grottoes there are also those of the *Pirate* with their famous *Victoria* lake. They were on display in the last century and considering their beauty it is to be regretted that they be closed.

Majorcan country girls.

Porto Cristo.

Manacor (50 kms. from *Palma*). The road goes past the villages of *Algaida* and its typical inns, *Montuiri* and its prehistoric remains and *Villafranca de Bonany*. At first the road stretches out in a rich area of vegetable gardens with hundreds of water pumping windmills up to the woods at *Xorrigo*. All along the road almond tree plantations dominate. They are the chief agricultural wealth of the island. At the beginning of February the white blossoms on the trees strikingly contrast with the green mantle of the farmed fields.

MANACOR (24.000 inh.). — Head town of a district. Prosperous and thriving agricultural town with a furniture making and artificial pearls industries. As to monuments we should mention the fair sized church and its very high bell tower which can be perceived from far away towering over the town. Next comes the former convent of *Sto. Domingo* dating from the 17th and 18th century, la *Torre de Ses Puntes* a 15th century monument displaying gothic *doublewindows (Finestres coronelles).* Out of over 40 windmills standing about the primitive town, only a few ruined towers are preserved.

In order to visit the grottoes we should proceed on our journey to *Porto Cristo* (12 kms. away), a fisherman's hamlet with a beach and a lively colony of summer holiday makers inns and restaurants. The famous grottoes are situated nearby.

Harbour of *Pollensa.*

Road to *Formentor - Porto Colom.*

Grottoes of *Drach*. Lake.

DRACH GROTTOES. — Piferrer called them the underground *Alhambra*. They have been known for a very long time and visitors have been admitted since the end of the past century. They stretch out for a length of over 2 kms. It is impossible to give an account of the number of halls or a description of the manifold features of the older part: the Black Cave, the Sultan Bath, the Drawing Room, the Purgatory, the Lake of Wonders also the Blue Caves and its Lake of Delights is one of the most beautiful spots inside the grottoes.

In 1896 Martel the great French speleologist sponsored by the Archduke Luis Salvador of Austria explored the famous lake which has been named after him since then. He discovered on the opposite bank the vast cave of the French. Lake Martel is 177 mtrs. long. 40 mtrs. wide on an average and 3 mtrs. deep. Visitors sail across the transparent still waters of the lake under a fantastic vault of stalactites electrically lit like the rest of the grottoes. The lighting was planned by enginneer Bohigas and has become impossible to criticise the lighting effects.

HAMS GROTTOES. — They were discovered in 1906 explored for years and have been admitting visitors for a few years. That is the reason why they retain their early fragile purity; smoke-giving torches being never used to light them.

← *Torrent de Pareis.*

← *Milinary Olive tree.*

Beach of *Porto Cristo*.

They are called *Hams* after the *Majorcan* word for *"hook"* on account of the great number of harpoon-shaped white, transparent stalactites in them. They stretch out for about 350 mtrs. and are electrically lit. Their chief features are the white transparent stalactites many of them joining the floor to the vault. Notwithstanding the beautifully and delicately worked details, there are vast halls such as the so called Imperial Palace of breath-taking grandeur, the round shaped Rest Room over 50 meters diameter, the Venetian sea is a lake, it is possible to sail across, and quite a number of smaller rooms, all of complicated and finely worked details.

ARTA (5.200 inh. and 20 kms. from *Manacor*). — Here is a town with a good number of stately and dignified houses bestowing on it an air of grandeur. The large sized church stands on a height dominating the town from that spot a flight of steps leads up to *San Salvador's* church situated on a small hill the village is leaning against, where some remains of the old ramparts are to be found, and which command a view of the whole district.

Some interesting megalithic monuments remains in the district. The most noteworthy are *Talaiot Cánova* 10 kms. away near *Colonia de San Pedro* and *Talaiot Pahisses* by the railway

Cala Ratjada.

Artá. Hermitage of *Betlem.*

Cala Bona.

station. Its gateway consists of huge bolders. A museum worthy of a visit has been founded with objects dug out nearby.

An interesting excursion could be carried out to the Hermitage of *Belén* (10 kms.). An oratory and a *Hostelry* stand there side by side and a beautiful view of the bay of *Alcudia* is afforded.

From *Artá* is easy to pay a visit to *Capdepera* (8 kms.) and nearby to the Castle and old fortress of the Middle Ages Oratory of Our Lady of Good Hope in the purest gothic art. In the mountains around dwarf palm trees are plentiful. Their plentiful palms are the raw material for the most important activity in the village: palm handwork.

At 2 kms. from *Capdepera* and 80 kms. from *Palma* the village of *Cala Ratjada* lies by the harbour and a handful of fisherman's houses. Nowadays it has turned into a touristic resort with up-to-date hotels and a numerous colony of holidaymakers in the summer time. March's Palace on an unmatched site should be mentioned. 2 kms. further on, we reach cape *Capdepera*, the easternmost point on the island with a first category lighthouse, on a craggy rock commanding the whole channel separating Majorca from Menorca. Ships sailing between France and Algeria ceaselessly sail these waters, their route precisely off that point.

Cala Millor.

Cala Millor.

Porto Cristo. S'Illot.

Artá. La Almudaina castle.

Capdepera and *Cala Ratjada* make out a vast area ot count-less rambles. Fine sandy beaches studded between huge cliffs are in great numbers (*Cala Gat, Cala Moll, Cala Gulla, Cala Mesquida,* etc.). On mount *Son Jaumells* one hour away there remains an old watchtower, one of those towers forming the defensive network of the island against the raids of pirates. The optic telegraph-post relaying communications to Menorca was set up there for a very long time until a submarine cable was laid.

On the *Son Servera* coast the beaches and coves situated between *Cabo del Pinar* and *Punta Amer* deserve mentioning. Between 3 to 5 kms. from the village we find *Cala Bona, Cala Millor, Port Nou, Port Vell, Es Ribell, Punta Rotja,* etc.

For the visit to *Artá* grottoes we may start from *Capde-pera* (8 kms.) or from *Artá* itself (10 kms.). The grottoes are situated between *Canyamel* and *Cap Vermell. Canyamel* is a fine creek perhaps rather a bay lined with a sandy beach adjoining thick groves of tall pines called *Es Pins de Ses Vegues,* this is where the grottoes restaurant stands. *Canyamel* estate farm-buildings consist of an old square embattled gothic tower close to the road.

Capdepera. Castle

Capdepera. La Esperanza Oratory.

Cala Ratjada.

Artá. Canyamel Tower

Entrance to the grottoes.

Artá. Beach of *Canyamel.*

ARTA GROTTOES. — The gateway is like a high vaulted mouth gaping over an enormous precipice onto the sea. The way up is by a masonry light of steps starting from the small square where the road finishes up. From the gateway we gaze upon one of those sights which so deeply impress the visitor that he is not likely to forget. The sea is seen from a very great height through the opening in the rock. The visit is carried on with all comfort on account of the firm track and electric lighting. They stretch out for about 300 mtrs. and have been considered by A Reclus as among the most beautiful in the world. They were known very long ago, explored and described by the eminent people who visited them. Faura y Sans says: "It is hardly possible to be concise on describing the wonderment caused by gazing at the supreme grandeur of the caves".

Their characteristic feature is a grandeur beyond any descriptive attempt. Though magistrally lit, on account of the great height, there exist places in the vault which can only be lit by search-lights. Among so many grand halls let us mention as outstanding the Hall of Columns; the Hall of the Queen of Columns in which a single column is 22 mtrs. high; Purgatory, Inferno Halls where an absolutely vertical arrete is 17 mtrs. high; the Theatre is another hall 30 mtrs. high and 10 mtrs. wide. In the latter hall one of the receses is the furthermost point from the entrance (310 mtrs.). The hall of Flags is 45 mtrs. high. At the end of the visit you are back to the entrance hall seeing the sunlight come through little by little, thus giving the visitor a deeply impressive view in contrast to what he had just seeing which makes it an unforgettable moment, an ever lasting one.

Having visited the caves this excursion is finished and we can return to *Palma* directly (81 kms.) without passing through *Manacor*. We can either take the road *Artá-San Lorenzo-Manacor* or another very beautiful: *Artá-Son Servera-San Lorenzo-Manacor*.

We can also return to *Palma* by following the above road to a point about 21 kms. from *Artá*, then taking a road to the left and following it to *Inca* (22 kms.) and from there to *Palma*. This road passes through *Muro*, a village in which we could make a stop. It has a beautiful church with a high gothic bell-tower and the ancient and typical house of *"Alomar"*, now converted into a museum of local crafts; there is a collection of many hand-tools which today, replaced by modern agricultural machinery, have fallen into complete disuse.

6th EXCURSION TO PETRA

This village is in the center of the island, 44 kms. from *Palma* and 4 kms. from the main *Palma-Manacor* road. Two kms. before arriving at the village there is the manor house of *Son Santandreu,* which has authentic Majorcan furnishing and a valuable collection of old fans of the best styles.

Petra is a village worthy of a visit for being the birthplace of Fray Junípero Serra. The history of the whole village revolves around this great Franciscan preacher who was born here on the 24th of November 1713, founder of the cities of Los Angeles, Monterrey, San Diego, San José and San Francisco in California. Preserved today is the XVII century monastery where he was formed. The names he gave to the today big cities of California were the names of the different chapels of the monastery. Also preserved is his birthplace in every detail which is an example of an ordinary Majorcan dwelling of the XVIII century, and also a typical winecellar. The parish church contains some gothic altar pieces and some notable dalmatics.

Recently a statue of the great preacher was erected in the main square, a museum founded and a centre of juniperian studies. In 1927 his statue was placed in the Hall of Fame in the Capitol, Washington, USA.

There is an interesting excursion from *Petra,* to the Sanctuary of *Bonany* (5 kms. from the village). The hermitage and hostelry stand on a hill 300 mtrs. high from which one can see the whole central plain of the island.

From *Petra* one can return by the same road to regain the *Palma-Manacor* road, or one can continue the Excursion by following the road to *Santa Margarita* and *Muro* where one can visit the interesting Craft Museum, and from there to *La Puebla.* Both villages have many irrigation mills and rich farmlands which last until one reaches the *Palma-Alcudia* road, 42 kms. (See 3rd excursion.)

← *Petra.* Interior of birthplace of Fray Junípero Serra.

Porto Colom.

Felanitx - Castle of Santueri.

Beach of *Porto Cristo.* →

Cala Ratjada. Beach of *Cala Gulla.* →

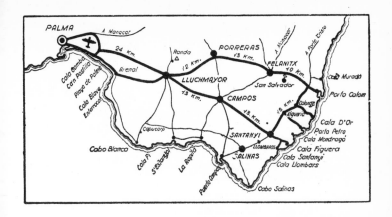

7th EXCURSION: PALMA - LLUCHMAYOR - PORRERAS - FELANITX AND PUIG DE SAN SALVADOR - SANTANYI AND CALA FIGUERA - CAMPOS - LLUCHMAYOR - PALMA

This excursion can be combined with the preceeding, starting from *Manacor* 12 kms. from *Felanitx*. There is also a direct road connecting *Porto Cristo* with *Porto Colom*.

There are several routes to go from *Palma* to *Lluchmayor*. For being the best and more cheerful, we recommend the road to *Can Pastilla* and from there the big avenue that borders the ocean *(playa de Palma)* up to *El Arenal*. Then directly to *Lluchmayor* (25 kms. from *Palma*), city of 12.000 inhabitants with an important shoemaking industry. At 12 kms. we go through *Porreras*, where you will enjoy visiting the church and admiring the valuable objects, among them a processional gothic cross proceeding from the Templars. From here there is an interesting excursion to the Sanctuary of *Montesión* (2 kms.) which was an old monastery with is cloister of irregular shape, chapel and lodging, all well preserved.

On our way east we find *Felanitx* 13 kms. away. It is an ancient town that has made important progress in recent years. Many imposing houses are to be found there and its church is quite remarkable on account of its size. It was built in the 12th century and restored in the 17th. One enters it by a wide flight of steps. In the square in front of the church stands *San-*

Felanitx. Cala Marsal.

ta Margarita fountain. *Felanitx* is a very important agricultural town and wine-growing centre together with a pork preserves industry.

An interesting excursion can be made to *Porto Colom* 12 kms. away — this is a small village with a safe and large, though shallow, harbour. However, the most interesting excursion which can be made is to the Sanctuary of *San Salvador* 4 kms. away by a good road. The sanctuary stands 500 m. high. This trip is recommended because it is both fine and easy. From the Sanctuary we have a fine panoramic view and the fact that we are on an isolated peak in the middle of the southern plain of the island enables us to see many villages, the immense stretch of the sea and the island of *Cabrera* away to the south.

At the Sanctuary stands a great hermitage founded in the 12th century with a vast hostelry and restaurant. In the first lateral chapel there is a magnificent Gothic altar-screen carved in stone — a remarkable work and worth seeing.

Another excursion which can be started from *Felanitx* (6 kms. away by road) or from *Puig de San Salvador* is the one to *Santueri* Castle. This is a medieval fortress with embattled towers splendidly situated in this *San Salvador* mountain group. Although less elevated, *Santueri,* being further to the south, dominates the whole southern plain of the island, the sea on two sides and the island of *Cabrera.* This is one of the oldest fortresses in Majorca. According to *Bover* it was built by the

179

Cala D'Or.

Cala D'Or.

Santanyi. Cala *Figuera.*

Romans and served as a defense for *Porto Colom, Porto Petro* and *Cala Llonga.* In the Middle Ages it withstood several sieges and in 1459 served as a prison for Charles of Navarre, Prince of Viana.

From *Felanitx* one can proceed directly to *Santanyi* (17 kms.) but to complete the southerly and easterly circuit it is better to go first to *Cala d'Or.* To do this, after visiting *San Salvador* we drive on the same road to *Porto Colom* and, one km. away from the village, we turn south past *L'Horta* and *Calonge* to *Cala d'Or* and *Cala Llonga.* From *Cala d'Or* we must return to *Palma* (62 kms.) driving once more past *Calonge* and *Alquería Blanca.* 12 kms. away we reach *Santanyi.* In its church is an organ of gigantic proportions which came from the Convent of *Santo Domingo* in *Palma.* There is also a Gothic chapel.

The most interesting feature at *Santanyi* is the excursion to the easterly coves 5 or 6 kms. from the latter. There is a marvellous ensemble consisting of *Cala Mondragó, Cala Figuera, Cala Santanyi, Cala Llombarts,* lined with thick pine woods and outdoing each other in picturesqueness. These solitary spots are among the most picturesque and beautiful on the whole Majorcan coast-line. At *Cala Figuera* stands a fisherman's hamlet and port, a modern settlement for holidays makers with up-to-date buildings, a restaurant and lodgings sharply contrasting with the rest.

Santanyi. Es Pontás.

Between *Cala Santanyi* and *Cala Llombarts* close to the coast there is *El Pontás* and impressive rock isolated off the shore in the shape of a bridge.

From *Santanyi* we can return to *Palma* directly (50 kms.) or round through *Ses Salinas* and *Port de Campos*. We motor through cultivated fields, the villages of *Campos* and *Lluchmayor* and reach at last *Palma*. This excursion, if the trip to *San Salvador* be included, has a total length of 145 kms.

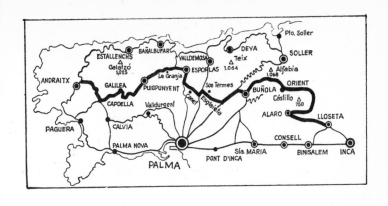

8th EXCURSION: PALMA - LLOSETA - ORIENT - BUÑOLA - S'ESGLAIETA - ESPORLAS - PUIGPUÑENT - GALILEA - ANDRAITX

"Spain is different" is the official slogan of tourist publicity. The scenery of Majorca is exceedingly varied, one can hardly find anywhere such richness of different landscapes, and beautiful places in such small area (3.600 km.²). The visitor will be able to see this himself if he has been in the excursions we have mentioned and also goes on those we are going to present to him. So far we have already seen 200 beaches most of them with buildings, provided with restaurants, bars, night clubs, etc., big blocks of hotels and apartments, of a modern dull style, that one finds all over the world; we have enjoyed the views of the Northern coast with its cliffs, and the immensity of the sea from strategic view points *(miradores)*. Among such heights stands out the great crevice of *Torrent de Pareis* and the cosy harbour of *Sóller*. We have also visited the *Drach* caves, finding large crowds everywhere we have been.

Lloseta. Main Square.

Orient.

Alaró in winter.

The following excursion is the opposite to all we have depicted. This will be an inland trip, through valleys and along mountain sides, we shall only see the sea from a long distance at the end of the excursion. We shall take sight of another Majorca, the quiet one, not yet invaded by bikinies, with no traffic difficulties no policemen to order you about, just beautiful landscapes, dotted with country houses some of them stately mansions, built in past centuries. We shall go through some small villages that still maintain their traditional way of living. We come across pine woods and tilled fields which in old days were planted with olive trees, substituted now by carob almonds, and fruit trees, etc. These lands were the main source of wealth of the island before the tourist industry began. We recommend this excursion to those who might be interested to see the contrast between the modern Majorca seen in previous excursions and this traditional one not yield to present modernization.

We leave *Palma* by the *Inca* road crossing *Pont d'Inca*, *Santa María*, *Consell*, and *Binisalem*, which has already been described in excursion 3. After going 24 kms. we turn to the left, and after 4 kms. more we arrive at *Lloseta*, where there is an important shoe industry. What is worth seeing is the church square, with *Ayamans* house, it has beautiful gardens.

Buñola.

The excursion in fact starts here, in *Lloseta*, where we proceed to *Alaró*, 8 kms. away, with its typical neighbourhood called *Las d'Amunds* one of the oldest in the island. There are also some shoe factories here. At some distance there is a castle, to which we have already refered in the chapter about the mountains: *Son Forteza, Solleric, Son Bergues, Son Grau, Son Antem, Banyols,* etc.

From *Alaró* the road runs up along the mountain side on which the castle stands. On the other side of the road is the mountain of *S'Alcadena*, passing through the estates *Son Curt, Son Cladera, y S'Olivaret*, finally reaching a height from where we have a beautiful view of the *Solleric* valley, with the mountains in the background. The road runs through olive fields and comes to *Orient*, a small hamlet 10 kms. above sea level. This is a starting point for many mountain walks, mentioned in the corresponding chapter. We continue along the valley and descend to *Buñola*, a railway station on the railway line between *Palma & Sóller*. Surrounded by mountains of which *Se Comuna* is the most interesting. There is a good road to the top where one can find a beautiful view of the island plain.

From *Buñola*, we take the *Palma-Sóller* road. After 14 kms. in the region of *C'an Penasso*, there is an old inn where the carts and carriages stopped to change horses on their way from *Palma* to *Sóller* and vice versa. After following this road 12

Puigpuñent.

more kms. we come across the gardens and mansions of *Alfabia* and *Raxa*, with their gardens and fountains, all of which have been described in excursion N. 2. We leave the *Palma-Sóller* road and take the road which passing through *Son Termes* leads to *S'Esglaieta* with its small chapel and small population, being 11 kms. away on the *Palma-Valldemosa* road. We leave this road, take the deviation which goes along the *Canet* Valley, at the entrance to which we can see some remarkable gardens, and magnificent steps and 5 kms. further on we find ourselves in the village of *Esporlas* which we ought to go through. Having done so we come to the estate known as *Sa Granje* (The Farm), well known for its mansion house, patio, gateway and gardens.

Here the road we should take goes off to the left towards *Puigpuñent* passing through *Soperne*, always in beautiful deserted countryside, with mountains on both sides. One of the most interesting being *Son Vic*, with its gardens and a small lake. At *Puigpuñent* one should definitely visit *Son Forteza*, 2 kms. away, with its very high waterfalls. This is the beginning of the *La Riera* the river, which flows out into the sea in the harbour of *Palma*, after flowing through the city. From *Puigpuñent* the road goes to *Galilea*, a peaceful place with its houses scattered on the hill sides, at the top there are some old windmills. From the top of this hill one can see the huge mountain *Galatzó*, more than 1.000 meters high. It is the first

Galilea.

time in this excursion that we can see the sea far away in the distance. The road continues through rough countryside until it reaches *Escapdella*, a village already showing signs of modern building. From here we continue through the *Coll de N'Esteve*, and after 10 kms. through plains, very varied countryside and interesting estates among which *Son Hortolá* and *Son Mas* stand out. Then we arrive at *Andraitx*, the end of the excursion. We have travelled about 70 kms. from *Lloseta* and about 100 from *Palma*.

Andraitx may be found in the 1st excursion, from there one can take all the trips mentioned in this excursion. There are several ways to come back to *Palma*. The shortest is to return to *Escapdellá* and then through *Calviá* and *Palma Nova* to *Palma*. Another way is taking the road from *Andraitx* direct to *Palma*. The longest way via *Estallenchs* and *Esporlas* is 52 kms.

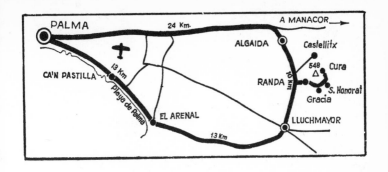

9th EXCURSION: MOUNT RANDA
(60 kms. round tour)

From *Palma* we motor along the road to *Manacor* as far as km. 22 where we turn right and on through the village of *Algaida*. 3 kms. away to the left a by-road leads to *Castellitx* 2 kms. away. There, we find an old oratory whose gate is a magnificent instance of romanic byzantines style unique in Majorca. According to some scholars that was the earliest christian temple to be erected after the conquest.

Motoring along the former road and 5 kms. away from *Algaida* there stands *Randa* a small satellite hamlet of the former on the sides of the mountain. The road which is to lead us up to the top starts there. 3 kms. away and 600 mtrs. high the oratory of *Cura* stands. There the great 13th century Majorcan scholar *Ramón Llull* settled for a time and wrote his major *Ars Magna*. Being quite isolated the mount is an excellent viewing place from which on clear days the whole plain of the island, the bays of *Palma* and *Alcudia* and island *Cabrera* are visible. An up-to-date and comfortable hostelry has been established there. It is run by monks of the Franciscan Order.

San Honorato's monastery stands 1'5 kms. away together with a small church. On the side of the mountain overlooking *Lluchmayor* the Oratory of *Gracia* stands. It was earlier situated under a huge rock. A modest hostelry can afford some kind of accomodation.

The way back to *Palma* can be through *Lluchmayor*. The route has already been described in Excursion 7.

Sanctuary of *Cura*

Sanctuary of *Gracia*.

Beach of *Ca'n Picafort*.

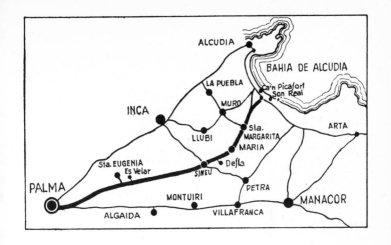

10th EXCURSION: PALMA - SINEU - MARIA DE LA SALUD
SANTA MARGARITA - CA'N PICAFORT

This excursion crosses the island through cultivated fields which make up Majorca's agricultural wealth and ending up in the tourist residential resort of *C'an Picafort*. We take the *Manacor* road from *Palma* and once outside the city we come to the ancient inn named *ca'n Blau*. Here we turn off to the left onto the *Camí Vell de Sineu* road. For the first few kms., there are fruit orchads, vegetable gardens and cow sheds. After 10 kilometers the prehistoric remains of *Es Velar*, lies close to the road, 33 kms. from *Palma* we arrive in *Sineu*.

Sineu is a village of 3.000 inhabitants, important for its agricultural industry and its traditional market held every Wednesday. Nearby is *Defla* with its mansion house, beautiful trees 100 years old and gothic tower with a window of the same style. King *Jaime II* built this village, and his residential palace, later converted into a convent which still exists today although completely disfigurated. The road we have been on, used to be known as the "royal road", one of the oldest in the island, built to cross the country between *Palma* and the royal palace.

Beach of *Ca'n Picafort.*

From *Sineu* we continue through *María de la Salud* and *Santa Margarita* until we reach *Ca'n Picafort* about 50 kms. from *Palma.* This town is situated in a large pine wood, in the middle of the bay of *Alcudia.* It is a nice resort, with large avenues, full of life in the summer months, it has a fantastic beach. A little more than one km. along the coast may be found the necropolis of *Son Real;* a prehistoric site of very great interest. In Majorca there are more than 40 urban areas, tourist residences with their beaches and green areas. In spite of the fact that *Ca'n Picafort* is one of the most important of these resorts, it has not a direct bus service to Palma as many other smaller ones have.

Ca'n Picafort is the end of the excursion. If one does not want to return to *Palma* the same way one can complete the journey many other ways. *Alcudia* and *Artá* are situated on practically the same road so one can return via either of these places. Also one can return via *Petra* (found in the 6th excursion) or via *Muro* where the *Alomar* museum may be found. This museum has a complete collection of hand made tools especially those used in the country. From *Muro* one can continue to *Inca* and from there to *Palma.*

MOUNTAINERING

The mountain range dominating the northern part of the island has nine peaks over 1.000 m. high. So many excursions can be undertaken that we shall have to limit our scope to a survey of the chief rambles based on the roads leading up to the mountain passes.

These excursions are another appealing feature to tourists fond of this sport and it shows Majorca not only can offer its delightful piny beaches with sumptuous hotels and guest houses but is not devoid of this other inducement either, so different, and little known in which it can compete with most famed mountain resorts.

Before the existence of modern ice factory introduced at the the beginning of this century, during winter the ice was made in the top of the mountain by collecting and storing the snow that was later brought down to the city. They still conserve, in those heights, the store rooms for the snow, constructed with four walls without roof that once filled and packed with

← *Torrent de Parels.*

← *Santa María.* Parrish church.

snow to the top, were covered with branches. To arrive there, a footpath exists along which the snow, stored after the snow falls, was brought down by packhorse to the nearest road. These pathways today nearly destroyed by the action of time, can still be used for the mountain excursions.

ASCENT OF PUIG MAJOR (1.445 m.). — This is the highest mountain on the island. From it one has a view towards the south of all the plain and villages, to the north the immensity of the sea. On a clear day one can see *Menorca, Ibiza* and *Cabrera*, and here are those who claim even to have seen Catalonia. The point of departure is from *Son Torrella* whose houses situated at over 1.000 meters above sea level, almost border on the *Sóller-Lluch* road. It is necessary to obtain a special permit for the ascent.

ASCENT OF PUIG DE MASSANELLA (1.349 m.). — This is Majorca's second mountain. Although the ascent can be made by several parts, the most practical starts from *El Guix* and *Coma Freda*, a state near the *Inca-Lluch* road and about 2 kms. before reaching the Monastery whose buildings are situated at a height of 500 mtrs. The path has been marked out by the local Majorcan Touring Club and the ascent can be done in fairly good conditions. From the summit we can behold the huge mass of *Puig Major* and easterly, the immense sea at the south, nothing interrupts the view of the plain with a great number of tiny villages.

Because of the easy access we recommend this excursion.

ASCENT TO L'OFRE (1.090 m.). — One has the choice of two places as points of departure. *Sóller* and *Orient*. Both paths eventually meet at the *Ofre* farm near a spring and one path can be chosen for the ascent and the other for the descent. One advantage for starting the ascent at *Orient* is that we can use the road up to *Comassema* at a height of 400 mtrs. then a path leads up to the "barrera" where we come across the trail from *Sóller*.

Leaving *Sóller* we go to *Biniaraitx* where the steep mule track begins. It winds up the side of the mountain having in sight the famous oranges groves. At *Las Barreras* (the Barriers), we leave the trail to climb the last 200 m. The most interesting feature is the view of *Sóller*, the valley and the high mountains bounding it, as well as a view of *Pla de Cuber* and the high peaks in the mountain range.

← The highest mountain of the island.

195

ASCENT TO THE SERRA DE ALFABIA (1.038 m.). — This is more than a mere peak, it is a true massif with crest and ridge several kilometers long — hence its name of *Serra* or saw. Although several paths exist, the most practical is the mule-track beginning 20,9 kms. from *Palma* on the *Palma-Sóller* road just before arriving at the *Coll*. We should keep on this until we can make the ascent to the summit but no trail is available for this. Continuing on our way we reach *Las Piquetas de S'Arrom* where there is a superb belvedere overlooking *Sóller*. Afterwards, by mule path we can get down to the town in an hours time.

ASCENT TO TEIX (1.064 m.). — Out of the nine highest summits on the island this one is the nearest to *Palma*. To carry out this excursion we can start from two quite different places. — *Valldemosa* or *Coll de Sóller* both at 400 m. high.

If we start from *Valldemosa* we walk up the trail to *Son Gual* and *Sa Coma* which was built on orders from the Archduke Luis Salvador — a much loved person in this island — and we go along it until just before arriving at the summit we find a level stretch more than a kilometer long. From there to the summit we must walk 200 m. more without a path. Here is the famous "Cadira del Rei en Jaume" or (Chair of King James) from which we enjoy a fine view of the whole island plain with the city of *Palma* and its great bay and, to the east the peaks of the northern range.

Down the trail which we had left to reach the top of the mountain, we descend and in half an hour reach the *Casas del Rei Sancho* King Sancho's Houses. This Majorcan king was said to suffer from asthma and went to the summit of the *Teix* where he would rest in the *Cadira* already mentioned. From here a cart track runs to the estate of the king *Sancho's* house one hour from there, situated by the *Sóller* to *Palma* road.

The ascents to *Tomir* and *Galatzó* and *Puig Roig* and to *Tessols Verts* unlike those mentioned above, have but a secondary interest and do not make up for the difficulties they present, in spite of the panoramas they offer.

ASCENT TO ALARO CASTLE (800 m.). — This is a very easy excursion which can be undertaken from two different points — *Orient* and *Alaró*. If we start from *Alaró* we walk up the cart-track which passes through *Son Penyaflor* and *Son Curt* as far as *Verger* from where we take the path to the castle. The journey lasts about 2 hours. We can carry this ex-

cursion on to the other flank of the mountain past *Son Bergues, S'Olivaret* and *Solleric*. Here is an oratory and hostelry dedicated to our Lady of Perpetual Succour; greatly regarded in the village.

The whole mountain constituted a fortress in medieval times. It was of considerable military value and was defended by embattled towers which still exist. In this castle *En Cabrit* and *En Brassa* — two of the heroes of Majorcan Independence — resisted stubbornly the forces of the invader Alfonso IV, king of Aragon and here, when he eventually stormed the castle, the two defenders were burn alive.

Although the mountain is easy to climb, the view it affords is magnificent.

CLIMBING TO "LAS GOBIAS DE LA ALQUERIA" (608 m.). This excursion however not of great importance, is very interesting. Because of the facility and the short time in which it can be undertaken we will put it among those which can be recommended on account of the splendid panorama we enjoy from the top of the mountain.

As starting point we will take *La Alquería* an splendid countryplace with its mansions, beautiful façade, cloister (courtyard) and gardens, situated on the road *Palma-Sóller* (km. 16). This country-house lies at a distance of 1,5 kms. from the railroad-station of *Buñola* (Palma-Sóller electric railway). From the very house begins a cart-track which at 4 kms. passes a height on which, one finds at the left an indicator for the path that leads to the top of the highest of the three peaks of "*Las Gobias*" situated on the supports of the *Teix*, to the south of this mountain and between this and the town.

In the vicinity of this peak there is a well. The way is always easy to follow, put in condition and marked as it is by the "Fomento del Turismo" where in the top has been built a magnificent mirador an splendid balcony from where one dominates the *Palma*-bay and the plain surrounding the town which lies at a distance in straight line, of about 12 kms. One needs less than two hours to reach it.

The descent can be carried out on the opposite side following the same cart-track that we had left before and that reaches the houses of *Muntanya*. From this place and on a small path one descends to *Pastoritx* situated in a valley with magnificent and typical mansions with gardens and a beautiful courtyard. From there we reach the village of *Valldemosa*. Taking this road descending from "*La Gobia*" is more than double the first one and is not so easy nor to be recommended.

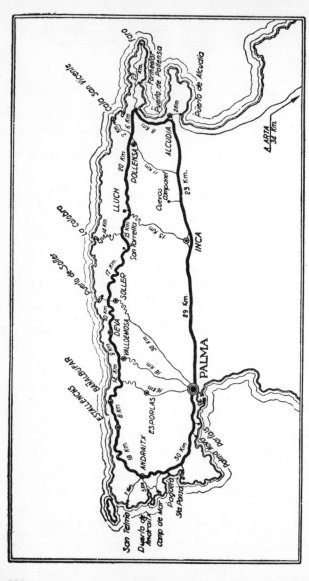

NORTHERN TOUR: PALMA - ANDRAITX - ESTALLENCHS BAÑALBUFAR - DEYA - SOLLER - LLUCH - POLLENSA PORT OF POLLENSA - ALCUDIA - PALMA (215 km.)

THE TOUR OF MAJORCA

We have been over the island in day excursions, taking the capital as a base, setting out in the morning and returning in the evening. For the most part, in spring or summer a morning or an afternoon is sufficient. The excursions made by coach are organized in this way, but the island can also be explored following other, more extensive itineraries, on other routes from which one hardly ever loses sight of the sea.

NORTHERN TOUR. — Excursions 1, 2, 3 and 4 can be made in a single tour, a drive of about 200 kms. We recommend doing it in two days, by comfortable stages. Moreover, from this same route there branch off other secondary ones leading to places of interest to tourists so that one always spends more time than expected. We shall omit the details of this itinerary in so far as they already have been described in previous excursions.

Leaving *Palma*, we make our way towards *Andraitx, Estallenchs* and *Bañalbúfar*, visiting *La Cartuja, Miramar, Deyá* and *Sóller* (see Excursion 2) going as far as the port itself. From *Sóller* we continue along a splendid modern highway towards *Son Torrella*, whose houses are situated at close on 1.000 meters above sea level. From here with special permission, one can go up to *Puig Mayor*, the highest point of the island. From *Son Torrella*, we continue by the *Gorg Blau*. One through this narrow passage we can leave the route and make a detour to *La Calobra* and visit the *Torrent de Pareis* (see Excursion 4). Back on the route again we go on to the Monastery of *Lluch* and from here to *Pollensa*. Towards the port of *Pollensa* and from there, along the seafront, make our way to *Alcudia* and its port.

Alcudia is the farthest point of this tour, and from here we return direct to *Palma* by an excellent highway, modernized throughout its entire length from which we can make a detour to visit the interesting caves of **Campanet**.

Palma Nova.

Harbour of *Andraitx.*

Beach of the port of Soller.

At *Palma* we end this round trip by which we obtain, with the minimum of travel, the maximum of interest in the island, the variety close to the sea along the edge of beaches and coves now crosses hills and goes through passes between the highest mountains, passing alternatively through stretches of dry, almost bare country, ending on the plain, so rich and well cultivated. The roads are the best on the island and some sections are of are hotels and restaurants, so that the trip can very easily recent construction. In all the spots indicated on the map there be divided into stages to suit individual tastes.

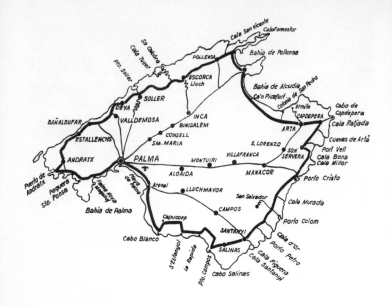

THE COMPLETE TOUR OF MAJORCA

In the previous tour we have covered the areas of the West and crossed the Northern mountain range of the island in all its extensiveness. But this can be covered in just one single and complete tour which would be about 300 kms. in all. It would be very difficult to do it all in just one day. However, on this tour there are more than 1.000 hotels and restaurants where anyone doing it in two or more days could stay. More days would be needed if one wished to visit the caves of *Artá*, *Drach* or *Dels Hams*, situated near to this excursion (see Excursion 5).

Leaving *Palma*, going Westwards, we pass through *Andraitx* and *Alcudia* on the same route as in the Northern tour. From the *Puerto de Alcudia*, instead of returning to *Palma*, we take the *Alcudia* road via *Son Serra de Marina* 34 kms. away. This road is not included in any of the previously described excursions. From *Artá* we go to *Santanyi* about 70 kms., along a badly surfaced road. Along the coastline numerous urbanizations have sprung up quite suddenly, in the summer, changing the quiet, isolated countryside with its wonderful beaches into a rich tourist area of chalets, apartments and all types of amusements.

Road to *La Calobra* & *Torrent de Pareis*.

Harbour of *Pollensa*.

Colonia de *Sant Jordi* (harbour of *Campos*).

From *Santanyi*, we can cut short the return journey, returning directly to *Palma* via *Campos, Lluchmayor* and *Playa de Palma* but if we want to complete it, we can carry on through the harbour of *Campos* or *Colonia de Sant Jordi* as far as *Cabo Blanco*. From here we go through *Arenal* to reach *Palma*. The same may be said for the Eastern coast of the island as far as developments and inflations of the land are concerned until we come to the city.

SEA TRIP ROUND THE ISLAND.— Here is a delightful tour which can be undertaken in the summer. Many pleasure yachts call at the port of *Palma*, at whose moorings we can count at times over 40 foreign yachts. Starting of from *Palma* we can anchor at the ports of *Andraitx, Sóller, Pollensa, Alcudia, Cala Ratjada, Porto Cristo, Porto Colom, Porto Petro, Cala Figuera, Cabrera* the port of *Campos* and finish up at *Palma*. We point out these anchoring places because yachtmen can rest assured of finding accommodation (except at *Cabrera*) and a fishermen's port for mooring safely any pleasure yacht. All of them are marked on the map and can serve as a basis for planning the different necessary stages of the trip.

Cala Pi.

Cabrera.

TRIP TO CABRERA ISLAND

Cabrera to the south of Majorca is separated from the Cape of *Salinas* by a strait 17 km. wide. It is 51 kms. from *Palma* and is connected with that city by a twice weekly boat service undertaken by a small steamer. The journey takes three hours. In no direction do the dimensions of the island exceed 7 kms. With *Conejera* and the neighbouring islets its total area is 1.800 hectares. Its loftiest point is *Puig de la Guardia* (172 m.). The island has cultivated areas and pine woods. Its greatest drawback is the existence of many wild goats. The climate is mild but too dry on account of the lack of rain. The island possesses and important lighthouse and the only inhabitants are the keepers and their families who are engaged in farming.

The outstanding feature of the island is its fine natural harbour of 50.000 sq. m. well sheltered from gales. Its mouth is 300 m. wide and is deep enough to allow large ships to enter and anchor.

The Castle, at the harbour entrance and built upon a rock 72 m. high is very interesting. It was built in the 14th century. The berber pirates captured it several times since the possession of the deserted island made it easier to attack Majorca. The castle is quite near the quay and from it, one has a fine view of the immense sea and the silhouette of Majorca.

We specially recommend the excursions to the *Cova Blava* (Blue Cave). The only way into this grotto is by sea in a small boat. It is impossible to disembark with safety. The water in the grotto is very deep and the bottom is covered with white sand. Light penetrating through the water is reflected on the white sand and inside the cave one sees this intense blue light. The grotto is but half an hour away from the quay.

Cabrera preserves a sad relic of the War of Independence. Of the French prisioners captured at the Battle of *Bailén*, more than 8.000 were interned here from 1809 to 1814. They suffered great hardships and but 3.600 returned home. In the port stands a small monument erected to their memory in 1849, by the French fleet under the Prince de Joinville's command.

There is nowhere to eat on the island so the tourist must provide himself with all he needs for the day. During the summer the fast and comfortable motor-cruiser *Carabela* makes the trip daily from *Palma* to *Cabrera*, visiting *La Cova Blava*, and on the return journey going right round the island.